349 Views o

# 349 VIEWS OF SCOTLAND

## DAVID SQUIRES

Whittles Publishing

Published by
**Whittles Publishing Ltd.,**
Dunbeath,
Caithness, KW6 6EG,
Scotland, UK
www.whittlespublishing.com

© 2016 David Squires

ISBN 978-184995-171-5

Printed by

# Contents

# Scottish view indicators by county

| | |
|---|---|
| Caithness | 6 |
| Sutherland | 8 |
| Ross and Cromarty | 29 |
| Inverness-shire | 33 |
| Nairnshire | 1 |
| Moray | 14 |
| Banffshire | 6 |
| Aberdeenshire | 21 |
| Kincardineshire | 5 |
| Angus | 7 |
| Perthshire | 21 |
| Argyll | 33 |
| Bute | 11 |
| Ayrshire | 21 |
| Renfrewshire | 8 |
| Dumbartonshire | 5 |
| Stirlingshire | 17 |
| Clackmannanshire | 4 |
| Kinross-shire | 2 |
| Fife | 13 |
| East Lothian | 12 |
| Midlothian | 15 |
| West Lothian | 6 |
| Lanarkshire | 4 |
| Peeblesshire | 5 |
| Selkirkshire | 0 |
| Berwickshire | 6 |
| Roxburghshire | 5 |
| Dumfriesshire | 5 |
| Kircudbrightshire | 12 |
| Wigtownshire | 4 |
| Shetland | 6 |
| Orkney | 4 |
| TOTAL | 349 |

# Introduction

About six years ago, I decided to compile a list of Scottish view indicators. That decision has resulted in this book. It consists of descriptions of 349 indicators, ranging in date from one installed at Ladies' Rock in Stirling in August 1890 to one installed at Cummings Park in Aberdeen in September 2013. In the course of researching the book, I have visited all the sites on the list.

It is not the first list of Scottish view indicators to have been compiled. In the 1930s, lists were published by the mountaineers James Parker and Ben Humble, and the chemist William Mair. A list also appeared in the *Scots Magazine* in 1959.

Nor am I the first person to make a trip around the indicators. In the summer of 1938, Ben Humble visited the majority of indicators that then stood in Scotland, reporting the results in a series of articles published in the Glasgow *Evening Times*. Humble's journey was my inspiration.

The list is hopefully self-explanatory. The indicators are arranged into counties; within each county they are arranged from North to South. The list includes devices which have been damaged, or removed completely, as well as those which are still useable. Sites which are marked as viewpoints on current Ordnance Survey maps are shown using the symbol ⚘. In almost all cases, grid references are readings from a GPS unit which were transcribed into a notebook while standing next to the indicator. Comments about the accuracy of indicators in terms of misidentified landscape features and the visibility or non-visibility of hills are based on comparison with digital panoramas. These were created using the software developed by Ulrich Deuschle and Michael Kosowsky.[1]

View indicators of four types have been included. The simplest is the **compass** design, where the directions of surrounding features are shown by means of radiating lines or arrows. An example is the indicator which stands at the summit of Lochnagar. With a **labelled image**, the device carries an image of the view as seen from the site of the indicator, on which features are named. The image is typically a hand-drawn sketch, but can also be a photograph or generated by computer. An example is the panel installed by the National Trust for Scotland at Inverewe. With a **bird's eye view**, the image is drawn not from the site of the indicator, but from a position some distance above the ground. An example is the panel at Warth Hill in Caithness. Finally, I have included **relief models**, such as

---

1   Ulrich Deuschle's program is available at *www.udeuschle.de* and Michael Kosowsky's at *www. heywhatsthat.com*

the device installed at Laggan Dam by the North British Aluminium Company in 1934.

An obvious question is whether the list is complete, in the sense of including all Scottish view indicators of the above four types. While considerable efforts have been taken to make the list as comprehensive as possible, it is likely that there are some which I have missed. Many indicators became known to me haphazardly: because someone mentioned them, or because I stumbled upon them either literally or through web searching. It is likely that there are others. This said, I believe that this is the most comprehensive list of Scottish indicators that has ever been compiled.

View indicators have been installed at some of the finest viewpoints in Scotland. The book will hopefully be of interest both to those who wish to see the country's most inspiring views and those who wish to know more about the history of the indicators. It is also likely that there will be some who will wish to visit them all. In fact, when William Mair published his list in 1939, a reviewer wrote:

instead of bagging a few more Munros, why not all the Indicators?[2]

In contrast to the Munros, there is currently no up-to-date list. Many are marked on Ordnance Survey maps, but by no means all.[3] Accordingly, a comprehensive catalogue will be an addition to the topographic literature.

Visiting these indicators has taken me to some wonderful places, and given me some wonderful days. Only a few of the best can be mentioned here. In Ross & Cromarty, I think of the Bealach na Ba, Balmacara Army Camp and Mam Ratagan. In Banffshire, the Bin of Cullen. In Argyll, Creag Bhan on the Isle of Gigha. In Buteshire, Barbay Hill on Great Cumbrae Island. In Stirlingshire, Ben Lomond and the Crown of the Wallace Monument. In Clackmannanshire, Ben Cleuch. In Fife, Norman's Law. In Midlothian, Allermuir Hill and on the coast of Kirkcudbrightshire, Castle Point.

But if I had to pick out the indicator which gave the most memorable experience of all, it would be the device which is on Foula, that speck of rock in Shetland with an official population of thirty one. Visiting that indicator involved a flight on a tiny plane and a night out in a bivvy bag, but the reward was great. The rock architecture of that island is unique.

## Humble's journey

Benjamin Hutchinson Humble was born in 1903 in Dumbarton: he was, as

---

2  *Cairngorm Club Journal*, Volume 15, Number 80, July 1939, p.80
3  By my count, 194 of the 349 indicators on the list are currently marked as viewpoints on Ordnance Survey maps.

he later put it, a Son of the Rock. He trained as a dentist, and one of his most striking early publications was a 1931 article in which he proposed a method by which dental evidence could be used to identify murderers and their victims. Several convictions have been obtained in British courts using the technique he proposed, and in one case (*Rex v. Ruxton*) the murderer was sent to the gallows as a result.[4]

But although his work was influential, Humble did not enjoy the routine practice of dentistry. To escape the drudgery of X-rays, extractions and fillings, he developed a second career as a writer and photographer. His passion was the Scottish hills, and above all, the Cuillin of Skye. After the success of his first two books, *Tramping in Skye* and *The Songs of Skye*, Humble agreed to write a regular column in the Glasgow *Evening Times*. His articles appeared each Saturday during the summer months every year from 1935 to 1939.

The series of articles from 1935, which appeared under the head 'The Open Road', formed the nucleus of his third book, *Wayfaring Around Scotland*. In 1936 came the series 'In the Footsteps of Hugh MacDonald', in which Humble revisited all the walks in the Victorian guidebook *Rambles Around Glasgow*. The premise of the 1937 series, 'Chronicles of the Wayfarers', was a visit to every youth hostel within easy access of Glasgow.

But of most interest to me was the series from 1938, 'Viewpoints of Scotland', describing the tour of view indicators he made in that year.[5] The first article begins:

> From where in all Scotland do you get the best view? No two persons would agree. One might want to see the rugged mountain ranges; another the fertile lowlands, villages, and rivers; a third the lochs and seas and isles of the west.
>
> Scotland can give all types of viewpoints, and Scotland appears to be the only country which, on a fairly extensive scale, has gone to the trouble of catering for visitors to its viewpoints.
>
> Scotland has at least 35 mountain or view indicators. A sixth of them are on the top of high mountains. There are no mountain-top indicators in England, Wales, and Ireland. There is no mention of mountain indicators in the new Encyclopaedia Brittanica or in the Oxford English Dictionary. And at Stirling there is a view indicator about 60 years old – one up for Scotland.[6]

4   Roy M. Humble, *The Voice of the Hills: The Story of Ben Humble MBE* (1995), pp.27-28.
5   The eighteen articles which form the 'Viewpoints of Scotland' series can be found in Ben Humble's scrap-books, now held by the National Library of Scotland in Edinburgh.
6   B.H. Humble, 'One of the Best Views in Scotland', *Evening Times*, 16 April 1938. The indicator at Ladies' Rock in Stirling, which was unveiled on 11 August 1890, was the first indicator to be installed in Scotland.

Over the next six months, Humble made weekly despatches to the *Evening Times*, visiting indicators on mountain tops, towers, Scout camps, parks, a golf course, a castle and a cemetery. The only drawback was the weather, which in the summer of 1938 was truly appalling, one of the wettest of the twentieth century. His encounter with Lochnagar was typical:

The wind was terrific. We could not stand upright. Photography was quite impossible and thick mist cut off all views.[7]

With Ben Macdhui, he was forced to admit defeat, retreating to the bothy at Corrour:

Our programme was to dump our packs, climb Ben Macdhui to have a look at the view indicator on its summit, and return to Corrour for the night. But, in the Cairngorms, the weather often decides one's programme. The mist came down and heavy rain came on. Corrour was indeed a haven, and we stayed there.[8]

The great event in Glasgow in the summer of 1938 was the Empire Exhibition at Bellahouston Park, visited by more than 12 million people during the six months it was open. Its symbolic focal point was a purpose-built steel viewing tower, 300 feet in height, known as the Tower of Empire. Humble was able to fit two articles about the Tower into his series seamlessly after he noticed that it had been equipped with a view indicator:

Like everything else connected with the Exhibition the view indicator is on a grand scale. It is in six sections of 6 feet by 18 inches and extends round the parapet of the upper balcony.[9]

By the time the concluding article of the series appeared in October, Humble had visited the majority of view indicators that then stood in Scotland:

The pilgrimage to view indicators has ended. It involved some strenuous journeys. Bad weather and lack of time foiled an attempt on Ben Macdhui, but Goatfell, Ben Lomond, Ben Cleuch, Lochnagar, and Ben Nevis were all climbed this summer – and not for the first time. The hilltops Tinto, Dumyat, Middle Eildon and Craigie Hill were easier jaunts, while the other visits were no more than afternoon walks…

---

7   B.H. Humble, 'Lochnagar – How the Indicator was Built', *Evening Times*, 28 May 1938
8   B.H. Humble, 'A Night in the Cairngorms', *Evening Times*, 4 June 1938
9   B.H. Humble, 'View from the Tower of Empire', *Evening Times*, 4 May 1938

The best viewpoint in Scotland? I would not care to say. Let each decide for himself; association and knowledge of the near-by country has much to do with one's choice. The most magnificent evening I had this summer was when I stayed by the Lyle Hill indicator for an hour and watched the sunset over the Argyllshire hills. No other viewpoint has such a grand foreground as the Tail of the Bank from there. My own favourite (I do not say the best) is the summit of Dumbarton Castle. How could it be otherwise with a Son of the Rock?[10]

At the time, Humble's project of providing descriptions and photographs of Scotland's view indicators perhaps appeared eccentric. But from a distance of more than seventy years, its documentary value has become clear. Many of the indicators he saw have since been replaced or removed; Humble's articles are in some cases the only record of what they looked like.

---

10  B.H. Humble, 'Complete List of View Indicators', Glasgow *Evening Times*, 1 October 1938

# CAITHNESS

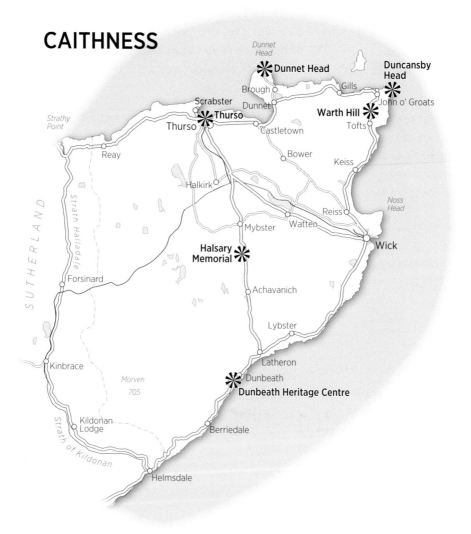

*Dunnet Head*

Dunnet Head

Duncansby Head

Brough

Gills

Scrabster

Dunnet

John o' Groats

Warth Hill

Thurso

Tofts

*Strathy Point*

Castletown

Reay

Bower

Keiss

*SUTHERLAND*

Halkirk

*Noss Head*

Reiss

Mybster

Watten

Halsary Memorial

Wick

Achavanich

Forsinard

Lybster

Latheron

Kinbrace

*Morven 705*

Dunbeath

Dunbeath Heritage Centre

*Strath Halladale*

Kildonan Lodge

Berriedale

*Strath of Kildonan*

Helmsdale

0                 10 miles

0                 10 km

# CAITHNESS

## Dunnet Head  

Three panels set on the walls of a paved viewing platform. Erected by Caithness District Council c.1980. Highland Council replaced the original panels with engraved Caithness stone slabs c.2008. At one time, there were telescopes on the platform, but these have been removed.

> Record for 'Easter Head, Dunnet Head: Cairn' on RCAHMS database (Canmore ID 8859)
>
> Personal communication, Drew McClelland, Highland Council, 12 April 2011

*Viewing platform at Dunnet Head. Photo taken 13/05/2010.*

## Duncansby Head

ND 404 733

Panel on a brick plinth. Erected by Caithness District Council c.1981. Highland Council replaced the original panel with an engraved Caithness stone slab c.2008.

Countryside Commission for Scotland, *Fourteenth Report*, 1981, p. 42

Personal communication, Drew McClelland, Highland Council, 12 April 2011

## Warth Hill

ND 372 702

Panel on a stone plinth. Erected by Highland Regional Council c.1988. Highland Council replaced the original panel with a framed paper chart in June 2006. It shows a bird's eye view of the landscape to the north, and some features (e.g. the Old Man of Hoy) are not visible from ground level. (Sea stack fanciers wishing to see The Old Man of Hoy from the Scottish mainland should visit Dunnet Head or Thurso.)

Countryside Commission for Scotland, *Twenty First Annual Report*, 1988, p. 61

Personal communication, Drew McClelland, Highland Council (I am grateful to Drew McClelland for supplying photos of the original panel).

## Thurso

ND 113 687

Bronze plate on a stone cube. Erected by Thurso Rotary Club in 1970.

*The Rotary Club's indicator at Thurso. Photo taken 28/06/2009.*

# Halsary Memorial  ND 173 485

Bronze plate on a stone cairn. Erected on the initiative of the aircraft enthusiast Dr Michael Diprose of Sheffield University and unveiled on Saturday, 29 August 1992. The cairn is a memorial to six airmen who died on a weather reconnaissance mission when their plane crashed on 1 February 1945. Creag Scalabsdale is hidden by Morven.

> John A. Kington & Peter G. Rackliff, *Even the Birds Were Walking*, 2000, pp.117–120

*The view from the Halsary Memorial, on the A9, has been significantly altered by the construction of Causeymire wind farm (2004). Photo taken 28/06/2009.*

# Dunbeath Heritage Centre ND 158 295

Metal plate mounted on a wall. The plate was installed by Dunbeath Preservation Trust in 1989, and is sited a few yards from a visitor centre, on the north-facing side. Maiden Pap and Morven are hidden by closer ground; Scaraben by houses.

> Countryside Commission for Scotland, *Twenty Second Report*, 1989, p. 59

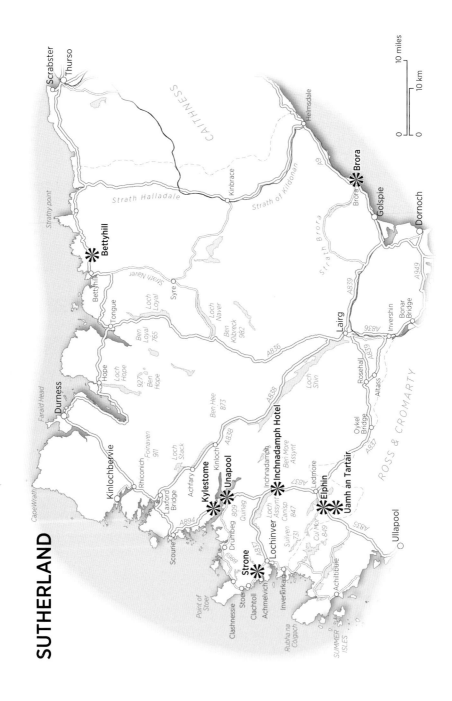

# SUTHERLAND

## Bettyhill

NC 748 619

Stone panel on a stone plinth. Erected by Bettyhill, Strathnavar and Altnahara Community Council c.2004. The peak identified as Arkle 787m is one of the tops of Foinaven; the peak identified as Beinn Ceannabeinne 383m is Meall Meadhonach 423m. The Community Council did not respond to an enquiry as to who was responsible for designing the panel.

Scottish Natural Heritage, *Facts and Figures*, 2003/04, p.184

## Kylestrome

NC 211 350

Laminated panel with a labelled photograph, mounted on a stone wall. There is also a coin-operated telescope (not working when I visited on 17 October 2013). One of the stopping points on the 'Rock Route', a motor car tour set up by Scottish Natural Heritage in 2001. Panels were installed at fifteen sites; five of these carry labelled landscape photographs and have been included here. In the winter of 2012/13, the original English-only panels were replaced with bilingual English and Gaelic ones. The peak identified as Beinn Aird da Loch 530m is Beinn Leoid West Top 729m.

SNH pamphlet, *The Story of Knockan Crag National Nature Reserve*, 2007

SNH, *The Rock Route Map*, available on the SNH website.

Sue Agnew, SNH, personal communication, 16 September 2013

## Unapool

NC 235 320

Laminated panel with a labelled photograph, mounted on a stone wall. One of the stopping points on the 'Rock Route' (see Kylestrome above).

## Strone

NC 075 255

Metal plate on a stone plinth. No consensus exists as to who installed this indicator, or its date. It is most likely that it was erected in the mid-1990s, as there is a viewpoint symbol at this location on the 1997 edition of the Ordnance Survey map *Northern Scotland*, but not the 1993 edition. A record in the HISP database shows that the device was in place by 17 August 1998, when it was visited by a Highland Council employee. They recorded the managing organisation as Scottish Natural Heritage. The plate depicted five of the Assynt hills. It was stolen in June 2007; the plinth remains.

> HISP database, ID 658, Highland Council, 1998 (I am grateful to Geoff Robson of Highland Council for supplying me with a copy of the HISP database on disc)
>
> 'Theft – Lochinver', press release on the Northern Constabulary's website

## Inchnadamph Hotel                                    NC 251 216

Laminated panel with a labelled photograph, mounted on a stone wall. One of the stopping points on the 'Rock Route' (see Kylestrome above). The panel will be found in the car park of a hotel.

*A panel near Inchnadamph Hotel identifies the hills to the North-West. Photo taken 17/10/2013.*

# Elphin

NC 212 106

Laminated panel with a labelled photograph, mounted on a stone wall. One of the stopping points on the 'Rock Route' (see Kylestrome above).

# Uamh an Tartair

NC 217 092

Engraved Caithness stone slab on a wooden support. Designed and installed by Tom Strang of Knockan in 2011.

Personal communication, Tom Strang, Knockan

# Brora

NC 909 039

Bronze plate on a stone plinth. Designed by the engineer Ian Colquhoun and erected by Sutherland County Council. According to local residents, the Brora direction indicator was installed in the late 1960s or early 1970s. It appears, marked with the word 'Indicator', on the 1971 edition of the 1:2,500 scale Ordnance Survey map. In a digital world, all the peaks on the plate are visible apart from Mormond Hill and Bennachie. In reality, the view north and west is obstructed by houses and hedges.

Obituary of Ian Colquhoun, *The Northern Times*, 7 May 2009

*The direction indicator at Brora. By way of a covert joke, the designer included on the plate 'Tigh Osda Arnagh'; this refers to Annie's Bar at the Sutherland Inn. Photo taken 28/06/2009.*

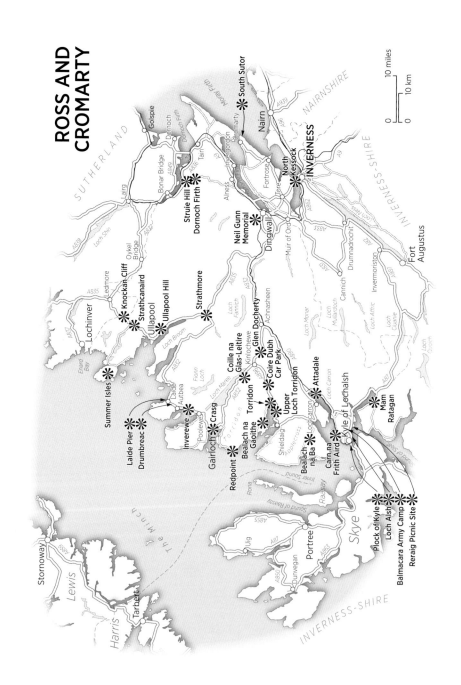

# ROSS AND CROMARTY

South Sutor

Nairn

NAIRNSHIRE

INVERNESS

North Kessock

Struie Hill
Dornoch Firth

Neil Gunn
Memorial

Dingwall

INVERNESS-SHIRE

Fort
Augustus

Knockan Cliff

Strathcanaird

Ullapool

Ullapool Hill

Strathmore

Summer Isles

Coille na
Glas-Leitire

Glen Docherty

Coire Dubh
Car Park

Laide Pier

Drumbreac

Inverewe

Gairloch Crasg

Upper
Loch Torridon

Attadale

Torridon

Redpoint

Bealach na
Gaoithe

Bealach
na Ba

Carn na
Frith Aird

Mam
Ratagan

Kyle of Lochalsh

Plock of Kyle

Loch Alsh

Balmacara Army Camp

Reraig Picnic Site

Skye

Portree

Dunvegan

Uig

INVERNESS-SHIRE

Stornoway

Lewis

Harris

Tarbett

The Minch

SUTHERLAND

Golspie

Dornoch

Bonar Bridge

Lairg

Loch Shin

Ledmore

Lochinver

Loch Broom

Aultbea

Poolewe

Shieldaig

Applecross

Loch Carron

10 miles

10 km

# Ross and Cromarty

## Summer Isles 

NB 984 132

Laminated panel on a stone plinth. Designed by the artist Janet Munslow and erected by Ross and Cromarty District Council, Coigach Community Council and Achiltiebuie Tourist Association. The designer believes it was installed c.1986/87. The peaks identified as the Cuillin of Skye are on the Scottish mainland.

Personal communication, Janet Munslow of Inverness

## Knockan Cliff 

NC 188 091

Steel plate on a plinth of local stone. Erected by the Automobile Association and unveiled on Tuesday, 25 April 1967. The AA plinth was removed in 2001 when the 'Rock Room', an unmanned visitor centre with a geological theme, was opened by Scottish Natural Heritage. The Rock Room included an indicator of different design: four laminated panels with a labelled outline of hills mounted on a stone wall. In the revamp of winter 2012/13, the panels were replaced by an outline of hills made from opaque glass.

'AA plinth unveiled near Ullapool', *The North Star*, 28 April 1967

SNH pamphlet, *The Story of Knockan Crag National Nature Reserve*, 2007

## Strathcanaird 

NC 157 035

Laminated panel with a labelled photograph, mounted on a stone wall. One of the stopping points on the 'Rock Route' (see Kylestrome above).

## Ullapool Hill 

NH 135 946

Metal disc on a stone cylinder. Designed by Ian Harrison, a student at Ullapool School, and erected by Rhidorroch Estate in 2001.

*Ullapool Hill: Woodland Walks*, leaflet published by Rhidorroch Estate, Forestry
Commision and Lochbroom Community

Personal communication, Jenny Scobie, Rhidorroch Estate

*The indicator at Ullapool Hill. Photo taken 19/06/2009.*

## Laide Pier                                        NG 903 925

The Laide Pier Viewpoint Indicator was described as providing an 'outline of
hills, heights and distances' by an employee of Highland Council who visited on
18 August 1998. They recorded the managing organisation as Highland Regional
Council. It is most likely the device was installed in the early 1990s as there is a
viewpoint symbol at this location on the 1993 edition of the Ordnance Survey
map *Northern Scotland*, but not on the 1989 edition. Exactly where it stood is
doubtful. The grid reference above – evidently an approximation – is from the
HISP database. When I visited on 19 June 2009, no physical evidence of an
indicator could be detected. Current Ordnance Survey maps have no viewpoint
symbol here.

HISP database, ID 346, Highland Council, 1998

## Drumbreac

NG 889 900

Metal plate on a stone lectern. William Macrae believes this indicator was installed by the District Council of Gairloch in the late 1960s. A photograph in Pennyfather's *Guide* shows that it was in place by 1975. By 18 August 1998, when the site was visited by a Highland Council employee, the plate was missing. When I visited on 19 June 2009, it was still missing; the plinth remained.

> Keith Pennyfather, *Guide to Countryside Interpretation: Part two*, 1975, plate 40
>
> HISP database, ID 345, Highland Council, 1998
>
> Personal communication, William Macrae, Gairloch Community Council

*The derelict Drumbreac view indicator, a mile from Aultbea. The plate has been missing since at least 1998. Photo taken 19/06/2009.*

## Struie Hill

NH 652 857

Bronze plate on a plinth of local stone. Erected by the Automobile Association and unveiled on Wednesday, 24 July 1957. A new plinth, with a steel AA plate, was installed when the lay-by was remodeled by Highland Regional Council c.1985. All the peaks on the plate are visible, but its orientation is about three degrees out

11

so that, for example, the arrow labelled Ben Horn points to Beinn Lunndaidh. The Struie Hill indicator has been a popular subject for postcard manufacturers.

'Viewpoint Plinth at Struie Hill', *Highland News*, 27 July 1957

Minutes of the Highland Regional Council Libraries & Leisure Services Committee, preliminary, 7 November 1985

## Inverewe

NG 871 848

Photograph overprinted with the names of distant peaks, mounted on a stone plinth. Erected by the National Trust for Scotland and opened by the Queen Mother on Tuesday, 14 May 1968. Alexander Gibson, who surveyed roadside facilities in Wester Ross for the Countryside Commission for Scotland in the summer of 1979, reported that the 'photographic panorama...has surface damage due, it is understood, to acid erosion from gull droppings'. Since then, the photograph has been replaced with a labelled drawing. When I visited on 19 June 2009, it was in good condition and guano free.

*The Queen Mother inaugurates the National Trust for Scotland's viewpoint at Inverewe. Source: National Trust for Scotland.*

'Wherever she goes she loves to meet people', *Press & Journal*, 15 May 1968

Keith Pennyfather, *Guide to Countryside Interpretation: Part two*, 1975, plate 41

Countryside Commission for Scotland, *Countryside Interpretation in Wester Ross*, 1984

## Dornoch Firth

NH 660 833

Framed paper chart with a labelled photograph, mounted on a low stone wall. Designed by Drew McClelland and erected by Highland Council in July 2007. The label Ben Tarvie is attached to the wrong hill.

Personal communication, Drew McClelland, Highland Council

## Strathmore

NH 195 784

Aluminium plate on a stone plinth. Designed by the artist Janet Munslow and erected by Highland Regional Council c.1986. The plate carried a labelled drawing of the view towards Loch Broom. When I visited on 19 June 2009, the plate was missing; the plinth remained. Highland Regional Council installed view indicators at Attadale, Strathmore and Glen Docherty following a report by the Countryside Commission for Scotland on countryside interpretation in Wester Ross.

Countryside Commission for Scotland, *Countryside Interpretation in Wester Ross*, 1984

Countryside Commission for Scotland, *Nineteenth Report*, 1986, p.55

Minutes of Highland Regional Council Libraries & Leisure Services Committee, 6 June 1985 (with accompanying paper dated 20 May 1985)

Personal communication, Janet Munslow of Inverness

## Crasg   NG 805 759

Metal plate on a stone table with five legs. The Crasg view indicator was erected by the District Council of Gairloch in 1968. Alexander Gibson, who visited in the summer of 1979, said that the view was represented by a line drawing. But a Highland Council employee who visited on 6 August 1998, described the indicator as having 'arrows to places only'. When I visited on 19 June 2009, the plate was missing; the plinth remained.

Countryside Commission for Scotland, *Countryside Interpretation in Wester Ross*, 1984

HISP database, ID 530, Highland Council, 1998

Personal communication, Maureen Barnie, Gairloch Community Council

## Redpoint   NG 731 692

Metal plate on a stone table. William Macrae believes this indicator was erected by the District Council of Gairloch in the late 1960s. The view is represented by a labelled drawing. Alexander Gibson complained that its 'effectiveness is limited by the lack of vertical exaggeration'. The peak identified as Fuar Tholl is Beinn an h-Eaglaise 736m. Fuar Tholl is not visible.

Countryside Commission for Scotland, *Countryside Interpretation in Wester Ross*, 1984

Personal communication, William Macrae, Gairloch Community Council.

## South Sutor   NH 807 671

Three laminated panels on a U-shaped stone plinth. Designed by the graphic designer Colin Dunn and erected by Cromarty Community Council in 1997. The project was the brainchild of the late Wilf Taylor, a retired teacher on the Community Council. Dunn tells me that he had heated discussions with Taylor about the identifications of the panels, but that it was Taylor who was ultimately responsible. Five of the nine natural land features named on the panels are misidentified.

> Personal communication, Colin Dunn formerly of Ceraph Design, 4 February 2011

*South Sutor viewpoint. Photo taken 07/10/2009.*

# Coille na Glas-Leitire                                    NG 997 649

Carved diagram mounted on a cairn. This indicator was erected by the Nature Conservancy Council c.1971 as a feature in a nature trail set up at the Beinn Eighe reserve. Footage in *Weir's Way* shows that by the late 1980s, the carved diagram was missing but the cairn remained. When I visited on 4 November 2009, this was still the situation.

> Countryside Commission for Scotland, *Fourth Report*, 1971 (picture of carved diagram on third page of illustrations after page 30)

Keith Pennyfather, *Guide to Countryside Interpretation: Part two*, 1975, plate 42 and 43

Tom Weir, *Weir's Way*, 'Wester Ross: Loch Maree' episode

## Neil Gunn Memorial         NH 518 609

A seven-sided stone construction, reminiscent of a large 50-pence piece, on which stylised depictions of some of the surrounding hills have been engraved. Erected by the Neil Gunn Trust and unveiled on Saturday, 31 October 1987 in the presence of around 200 people. It will be found about ten yards west of an obelisk which was installed at the same time. Neil Gunn rented the nearby Brae farm house in the forties and wrote some of his most celebrated books there including *The Silver Darlings*.

'Belated Honouring of Neil Gunn – Scotland's Leading Novelist', *Ross-shire Journal*, 12 November 1987

*The view indicator at the Neil Gunn Memorial. Photo taken 27/06/2009.*

## Glen Docherty        NH 066 593

Aluminium plate on a stone plinth. Designed by Janet Munslow and erected by Highland Regional Council c.1986. The plate carried a labelled drawing of the view towards Loch Maree. When I visited on 19 June 2009, the plate was missing, but the plinth remained. In September 2012, Highland Council Planning & Development Service removed the plinth and installed a laminated panel on a plinth a few yards from the site of the original. The new panel does not identify any of the hills.

Minutes of Highland Regional Council Libraries & Leisure Services
Committee, 6 June 1985 (with accompanying paper dated 20 May 1985)
Countryside Commission for Scotland, *Nineteenth Report*, 1986, p.55

## Bealach na Gaoithe                     NG 827 587

Sculpted relief model, cast in urethane resin and mounted on a plinth of local stone. Designed by Hamish Rose and erected by the Torridon Millennium Committee in 2001. Beinn Eighe 1009m is not visible.

'A Better View', *Nessie's Loch Ness Times* (online newspaper), 28 July 2001, Issue 242

*The Bealach na Gaoithe viewpoint looks across Upper Loch
Torridon to the hills beyond. Photo taken 19/06/2009.*

# Coire Dubh Car Park                                    NG 957 568

Laminated panel on a wooden block. Erected by the National Trust for Scotland in 2004/05. The labelled drawing of hills is similar in style to the panel at Torridon (see below).

> Personal communication, Ian Riches, NTS Archivist.

# Torridon                                               NG 896 564

Laminated panel on a wooden block. Erected by the National Trust for Scotland in 2004/05.

> Personal communication, Ian Riches, NTS Archivist.

# Upper Loch Torridon                                    NG 865 542

A panel showing Torridon mountains was found at this site by a Highland Council employee who visited on 26 July 1998. They recorded the managing organisation as Torridon & Kinlochewe Community Council. The date of installation is most likely to have been the early 1980s as there is a viewpoint symbol at this location on the 1984 edition of the Ordnance Survey map *Northern Scotland*, but no mention of an indicator by Alexander Gibson who visited the site in 1979. The original panel was replaced in 2007 by Scottish Natural Heritage. The new panel, which was designed by James Carter, has a labelled drawing of the peaks to the north and is set on a boulder.

> Countryside Commission for Scotland, *Countryside Interpretation in Wester Ross*, 1984
>
> HISP database, ID 518, Highland Council, 1998
>
> Personal communication, Alistair Milligan, Ross Associates

# North Kessock                                          NH 656 479

Aluminium plate on a stone plinth. Designed by Janet Munslow and erected by Highland Regional Council c.1982 in connection with the opening of North Kessock bridge. The designer told me that the plate carried a labelled drawing of the view across the Beauly Firth. When I visited on 20 May 2009, the plate was missing; the plinth remained. The ten figure grid reference from my GPS unit was NH 65621 47949. When I re-visited on 8 November 2013, the plinth had been removed.

Minutes of Highland Regional Council Leisure & Recreation Committee, 11
June 1981

Personal communication, Janet Munslow of Inverness

*The derelict North Kessock indicator. Since this photo was
taken (20/05/2009), the plinth has been removed.*

## Bealach na Ba   NG 774 425

Steel plate on a plinth of local stone. Erected by the Automobile Association and
unveiled on Wednesday, 5 July 1978. Alexander Gibson, who visited the following
year, found that the plate 'has unfortunately been misaligned so that the spokes
do not, in fact, point towards the features referred to'. The plate has perhaps been
remounted since then, as its orientation is no worse than many others. However,
three of the features on the plate are not visible, the lines of sight being blocked
by a mound located about 200 metres north-west of the plinth. Had the plinth
been sited on this mound, every feature would have been visible.

'AA viewpoint unveiled at Bealach na Ba', *Ross-shire Journal*, 7 July 1978

Countryside Commission for Scotland, *Countryside Interpretation in Wester Ross*,
1984

# Attadale                                        NG 925 396

Aluminium plate on a stone plinth. The plate has a labelled drawing of the view across Loch Carron. Designed by Janet Munslow and erected by Highland Regional Council c.1986. On some old Ordnance Survey maps, this site is marked by a viewpoint symbol.

> Minutes of Highland Regional Council Libraries & Leisure Services
> Committee, 6 June 1985 (with accompanying paper dated 20 May 1985)
> Countryside Commission for Scotland, *Nineteenth Report*, 1986, p.55

# Carn na Frith Aird                              NG 800 339

Triangular chart on a stone cairn. Erected by the National Trust for Scotland c.1998. Rum is visible, but appears over the top of Skye and not where shown.

> Personal communication, Iain Turnbull, NTS.

# Balmacara Army Camp                             NG 810 276

Iain Turnbull describes the indicator which stood here as a 'wooden construction with three panels made of Perspex/plastic, designed and erected by NTS'. It is most likely it was installed c.1988 when the Countryside Commission for Scotland gave a grant to the National Trust for Scotland for two viewpoint indicators at Balmacara. The device was removed c.1996. When I visited on 17 June 2009, except perhaps for a wooden post, no physical evidence of it remained.

> Countryside Commission for Scotland, *Twenty First Report*, 1988, p.62
> Personal communication, Iain Turnbull, NTS

# Plock of Kyle                                   NG 756 273

Bronze plate mounted on the wall of a viewing platform. Erected by Ross & Cromarty Council c.1974. The labelled outline of hills on the bronze plate has an unusually narrow field of view (about 30 degrees) and Alexander Gibson felt that it deals 'inadequately with the superb panorama at this site, since it covers only the mountains of south and central Skye and ignores all to the east and north'. In 2006, Highland Council installed a framed paper chart sited a few yards from the bronze plate. This has a wider field of view (about 150 degrees) but still ignores the east and north. Both the bronze plate and the paper chart were present when I visited on 17 June 2009.

Countryside Commission for Scotland, *Seventh Report*, 1974, p.40

Countryside Commission for Scotland, *Countryside Interpretation in Wester Ross*, 1984

*Secrets in the landscape*, Highland Council booklet

## Loch Alsh

NG 772 272

In the summer of 1979 Alexander Gibson found a 'vandalised view indicator' at this lay-by. Nothing has been traced as to the installer or date of this device. Highland Council installed a framed paper chart here in July 2003. This modern chart was designed by Drew McClelland. The peak on Skye identified as Sgurr na Coinnich is Beinn na Caillich 732m; the peak identified as one of the Five Sisters is Sgurr an Airgid 841m. None of the Five Sisters are visible.

Countryside Commission for Scotland, *Countryside Interpretation in Wester Ross*, 1984

Personal communication, Drew McClelland, Highland Council

## Reraig Picnic Site

NG 814 271

Panel mounted on a metal frame. Erected by the National Trust for Scotland c.1998.

HISP database, ID 751, Highland Council, 1998

Personal communication, Iain Turnbull, NTS

## Mam Ratagan

NG 904 198

Metal plate on a stone plinth. Erected by South-West District Council in 1972.

Countryside Commission for Scotland, *Fifth Report*, 1972, p. 4

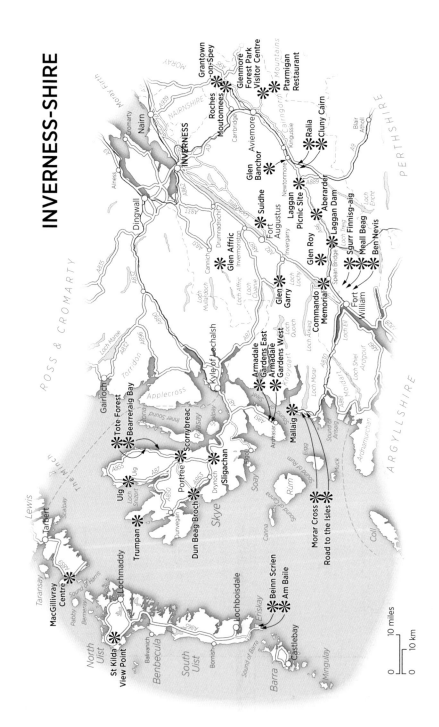

# INVERNESS-SHIRE

# INVERNESS-SHIRE

## MacGillivray Centre                                         NF 989 902

Granite slab on a stone plinth. There is also a pair of binoculars. These facilities will
be found a few yards from an unmanned museum dedicated to the naturalist William MacGillivray. The museum was built by a team of trainees with funding from
Western Isles Council and Scottish Natural Heritage, and opened in July 1998. Unfortunately it is not always clear which label is attached to which landscape feature.

## St. Kilda Viewpoint                                         NF 747 714

Two stone panels set onto the walls of a square viewing platform. Designed by
Donald Ferguson of Houghary, erected by the North Uist Partnership and unveiled
on Saturday, 29 August 2009. Some of the preparations for the installation of
this facility were recorded in an episode of *Monty Hall's Great Hebridean Escape*,
which first aired on BBC2. Apart from the panels, there is also a telescope.

   *Latha Hiort - St.Kilda Day,* leaflet available on the St.Kilda webpage of the NTS

*The St. Kilda Viewpoint on North Uist. A clear day is needed to see St.Kilda,
which is more than forty miles to the west. Photo taken 10/06/2010*

# Uig

NG 385 653

John Murray describes the device which stood here as 'a metal thin long plate which was on a wooden stand and showed the features of Waternish, The Uists, Harris and Lewis.' It was erected by Kilmuir Community Council in conjunction with Highland Regional Council c.1990. There was also a coin-operated telescope. The indicator and telescope survived until 25 August 1998, when they were visited by a Highland Council employee, but disappeared shortly afterwards. When I visited on 18 June 2009, there was no physical evidence of either.

HISP database, ID 286, Highland Council, 1998

Personal communication, John Murray, Kilmuir Community Council

# Trumpan

NG 224 612

Plastic covered paper chart on a stone plinth. Erected by Waternish Community Council in 2003. The peak identified as North Lee is South Lee; the peak identified as South Lee is Burrival. Waternish Community Council was unable to supply any information as to who was responsible for designing the chart.

Personal communication, John Phillips, Highland Council, 10 January 2011

*The Trumpan view indicator on Skye looks across to the Outer Hebrides. Photo taken 10/02/2011.*

# Tote Forest 🔆 NG 520 577

Two large slabs of synthetic stone mounted on separate stone plinths. Designed by Peter McDermott and erected by the Staffin Community Trust in summer 2008. The drawings on the slabs were based on photographs. The peak identified as An Teallach is Beinn Ghobhlach; the peak identified as Ben Tianavaig is Fiurnean; the peak identified as Slioch is part of Baosbheinn. Slioch is not visible. Meike Schmidt told me that 'the peaks were identified by several local people including a geographer and an outdoor guide'. An enquiry as to the names of these individuals was met with refusal.

> Personal communications, Meike Schmidt, Staffin Community Trust, 2 January 2010 and Peter McDermott, 4 January 2010

# Ardersier Common NH 778 556

Laminated panel mounted on a rock. Designed by Edward Garden Graphic Design of Dingwall and erected by Highland Council in 2002. The peak identified as Mount Eagle is the Hill of Fortrose. Mount Eagle is not visible.

> Interpretation Survey 2005–2010, Excel spreadsheet supplied by Jacquie Barbour, Highland Council

# Bearreraig Bay 🔆 NG 517 524

Laminated panels installed on three stone plinths. Erected by Highland Council in 1999. One of the panels carries an annotated sketch of the view.

> Personal communication, Rhoda Davidson, Scottish Natural Heritage, 5 November 2013

# Scorrybreac NG 490 437

Bronze plate, 36 inches by 18 inches, mounted on a stone plinth. Installed by the Clan MacNicol and unveiled on Saturday, 4 October 2008. The cairn is a memorial to Hammond Burke Nicholson (1917–2007), an executive in the Coca-Cola corporation, and his wife Juliet. Four of the Black Cuillin peaks are misidentified.

> *Scorrybreac: the Journal of Clan MacNicol*, Volume 25 number 2, December 2009, p.16

*The Scorrybreac view indicator near Portree. Photo taken 20/09/2013.*

## Dun Beag Broch

NG 337 384

Metal plate on a stone plinth. Designed by Janet Munslow and erected by Highland Regional Council c.1988. The peak identified as Beinn Bhreac is something else, probably Preshal Beg. Beinn Bhreac is not visible.

Countryside Commission for Scotland, *Twenty First Annual Report*, 1988, p. 61

Personal communication, Janet Munslow of Inverness

## Sligachan

NG 485 298

Metal plate on a stone plinth. Erected by the Skye and Lochalsh Footpath Initiative c.2000. It will be found a few yards from Sligachan Hotel.

Personal communication, Stephen Varwell, SNH, 2 December 2011

# Glen Affric                                      NH 276 275

Framed paper chart on a stone cube. Erected by the Forestry Commission in 1994. On 25 June 2013, the Commission replaced the original device with a design in which the western horizon is represented by carved wooden planks. These are mounted on a metal frame. The peak identified as Carn Eighe is Mam Sodhail; the peak identified as Mam Sodhail is Mullach Cadha Rainich. Carn Eighe is not visible. Access to the viewpoint is by means of a stone staircase signed from a forest track.

> Personal communication, Jonathan Taylor, Forestry Commission, 23 September 2013.

# Beinn Scrien                                     NF 795 112

Metal disc mounted on top of an Ordnance Survey triangulation pillar. Designed by Michael Cross and erected by Eriskay Community Council. The disc is dated 2003; it was fixed to the triangulation pillar by the designer on Monday, 12 April 2004. Local children cheered and clapped as the last screw was secured. The hill is now called Beinn Sciathan on Ordnance Survey maps.

> 'Topograph', *Stornoway Gazette*, 23 April 2004
>
> Personal communication, Michael Cross, Eriskay Community Council, 10 April 2009

# Am Baile                                         NF 788 110

Wooden carving mounted on a stone semi-circle. Michael Cross told me he thought this indicator was erected privately in the late 1990s.

> Personal communication, Michael Cross, Eriskay Community Council, 10 April 2009

# Suidhe                                           NH 449 105

Panel mounted on a boulder. Erected by Highland Regional Council c.1988 and renewed by Highland Council in April 2000. The peak identified as Tom na Croich 450m is Creag nan Clag 407m.

> Countryside Commission for Scotland, *Twenty First Annual Report*, 1988, p. 61

*The Suidhe viewpoint on the B862. Photo taken 27/06/2009.*

## Glenmore Forest Park Visitor Centre                NH 977 097

Bronze plate on a stone plinth. Presented by former pupils and staff of Elgin Academy and unveiled on Friday, 29 September 2000. It will be found on the south facing side of a Visitor Centre. A memorial to two men who ran school camps after the Second World War in a nearby timber hut (now demolished).

> 'Pair who loved the Cairngorms to get memorial', *The Northern Scot*, 6 October 2000

## Ptarmigan Restaurant                NJ 004 048

Four panels with labelled photographs mounted on the wall of a viewing terrace. The photographs were taken by Andy Gray in 2002. Erected by CairnGorm Mountain Limited, the operating company of the Cairngorm funicular. The viewing terrace can be accessed either by taking the funicular or by walking up the hill. The peak identified as Maol Chean-dearg 950m is An Ruadh-stac 892m; the peak identified as Beinn Tharsuinn 863m is Sgurr na Conbhaire 900m; the peak identified as Beinn Bhreac Mhor 807m is Carn Ghriogair 806m.

# Armadale Gardens East

NG 643 047

Panel on a stone plinth. Erected by the Clan Donald Land Trust c.1980 and renewed c.1994. The labels for Sgurr Coire Choinnichean 796m and Meall Buidhe 946m are attached to the wrong peaks.

Countryside Commission for Scotland, *Thirteenth Report*, 1980, p. 40

Personal communication, Rhoda Davidson, SNH, 4 May 2011

# Armadale Gardens West

NG 641 046

Panel set on a stone wall. Erected by the Clan Donald Land Trust c.1980 and renewed c.1994. Three of the ten peaks named on the panel are misidentified. Carn Mor 829m, Beinn Odhar 882m and Sgurr Dhomhuill Mor 713m are all hidden by closer ground.

*Two panels at Armadale Gardens on Skye carry labelled drawings of the view looking back to the Scottish mainland. This is the western one. Photo taken 23/02/2010.*

# Glen Garry

NH 211 028

Metal disc on a stone plinth. Erected by the Automobile Association in 1984.
A photograph on Flickr suggests that the disc survived until at least 8 February
2006. When I visited on 17 June 2009, the disc was missing; the plinth remained.

'Mountains', photo by Commander Holmes on Flickr (shows disc)

# Glen Banchor

NN 702 996

Bronze plate mounted on a boulder. Erected by the Newtonmore Community
Woodland Trust in December 1999 to mark the Millennium. The plate is a
feature on the 'Wildcat Trail'.

Newtonmore, five page brochure on the Newtonmore Community Woodland
Trust on the Forestry Commission website.

Personal communication, Colin Glennie (who installed the plate), 27 January
2010

# Mallaig

NM 680 972

Framed paper chart on metal legs. Designed by Drew McClelland and erected by
Highland Council in January 2005. The chart is set on a paved viewing platform
a few yards from the sea.

Personal communication, Drew McClelland, Highland Council

# Ralia

NN 699 968

Metal disc on a stone cylinder. Donated by the Bank of Scotland. HBOS, which
now owns the Bank of Scotland, could provide no information as to its designer
or date. It is most likely that the indicator was installed in the mid-1990s as
there is a viewpoint symbol at this location on the 1997 edition of the Ordnance
Survey map Northern Scotland, but not the 1993 edition.

# Laggan Picnic Site

NN 613 944

Plastic covered paper chart on a stone plinth. Erected by Highland Council in
March 2003. This site gives a view of the Cluny Macpherson monument, a stone
obelisk on a peak about a mile to the south. The name of the peak on which

this monument stands is rather variable, being called Carn Dearg on this chart, Creag Bhuidhe on Ordnance Survey maps and Creag Ruadh on the Cluny Cairn indicator (see below).

## Cluny Cairn                                              NN 677 941

Metal disc on a boulder. Erected by the Clan Macpherson Association and unveiled on Sunday, 4 August 1996. The opening ceremony was attended by more than 400 people including bagpipers. Opera singer George Macpherson led the gathering in a rendition of Psalm 121, 'I to the hills will lift mine eyes'. The disc is sited a few yards from a cairn which was built at the same time. Beinn a'Chrasgain 828m is not visible.

> *Creag Dubh: The Annual of the Clan Macpherson Association*, Highland Printers: Inverness, Number 49, 1997

*The indicator at the Cluny Cairn memorial.*
*Photo taken 11/12/2010.*

# Morar Cross

NM 679 927

Stainless steel plate on a stone plinth. Designed by Pat Ritchie and Archie MacLellan; erected by Morar Community Council and Highland Regional Council. At the unveiling ceremony of Tuesday, 7 July 1987, a crowd of 56 were encouraged to sing 'The Road to the Isles' and 'The Silver Sands of Morar'. When I visited on 16 June 2009, the plate was missing; the plinth remained. It was installed a few yards from a 17-foot high cross, originally set up in the nineteenth century.

> P. Galbraith, *The Morar Cross: A Brief History of the Cross and the Morar Church*, 15 page booklet.

# Road to the Isles

NM 671 910

Metal plate on a stone cube. Erected by the Scottish Executive in connection with the doubling of a section of the A830 in 2004. As is perhaps implied by the design of the plate, while Rum and Skye are visible from here, the islands of Muck, Eigg and Canna are not.

> 'Three Down, One to Go', *West Word*, April 2004 edition

*This indicator on the Road to the Isles (A830) looks west to Rum and Skye. Photo taken 20/02/2011*

# Aberarder 🔆 NN 482 872

When the Nature Conservancy Council built a car park at Aberarder c.1986 they installed a panel with a labelled drawing of the hills to the north on top of the surrounding stone wall. This is briefly seen in the episode of *The Munro Show* (broadcast 1991) in which Muriel Gray climbs Creag Megaidh. Of the two panels which Gray refers to as 'these little guides' it is the one on the left. The original panel was replaced with one of similar design by Scottish Natural Heritage c.1997. The SNH panel was mounted on a wooden stand rather than the wall, and was still in place when I visited on 16 June 2009. When I revisited on 11 December 2010, it had been removed to allow the car park to be enlarged.

> HISP database, ID 1352, Highland Council, 1998
>
> 'Creag Meagaidh National Nature Reserve', photo by Colin Kinnear taken 2008 on Geograph (SNH panel)

# Glen Roy 🔆 NN 298 853

Panel on a stone plinth. Erected by Scottish Natural Heritage in 1997.

> Personal communication, Martin Faulkner, SNH, 6 January 2011

# Commando Memorial 🔆 NN 208 823

Bronze plate on a stone cube. It is sited about fifteen yards east of a statue of three Commandos. Unveiled by the Queen Mother in September 1952. The peak identified as Beinn Bhan 2750 ft is one of the Grey Corries Munro tops, most likely Stob Corrie na Ceannain 3684 ft.

# Laggan Dam 🔆 NN 371 808

Relief model in bronze and enamel on a stone plinth. Erected by the North British Aluminium Company in 1934.

# Sgurr Finnisg-aig 🔆 NN 188 762

Panel on a stone cairn. One of a pair with Meall Beag, it was erected by Nevis Range Development Company c.1998. The panel survived until at least 28 April 2009, but when I visited on 1 March 2010, it was missing. The cairn remained.

*The indicator at the Commando Memorial, Spean Bridge. Photo taken 16/06/2009.*

The spelling Sgurr Finnisg-aig was used on the panel; on current Ordnance Survey maps the peak is called Sgurr Finniosgaig.

HISP database, ID 1372, Highland Council, 1998

Scottish Natural Heritage, *Facts and Figures*, 2000/01, p.160

Personal communication, Davie Austin, Nevis Range Development Co, 28 April 2009 (I am grateful to Davie Austin for supplying me with photos of the panel)

*A panel at the Sgurr Finnisg–aig viewpoint gave directions for the surrounding peaks. Since this photo was taken (28/04/2009), the panel has been stolen.*

# Meall Beag  ⁂     NN 177 753

Panel on a stone cairn. Erected by Nevis Range Development Company c.1998.

HISP database, ID 1373, Highland Council, 1998

# Ben Nevis

NN 166 713

Doulton stoneware disc on a cylinder of local stone with a cap of Aberdeen granite. Designed by James A. Parker and erected by the Scottish Mountaineering Club. Thirty people ascended the hill in thick mist and heavy rain for the unveiling ceremony on Sunday, 7 August 1927. R.R. Elton, Harry MacRobert and E.C. Thomson of the SMC made the ascent via the Tower Ridge, a rock climb on the eastern cliffs.

Some uncertainty surrounds the question of when the disc disappeared. Ken Crocket has written that it was destroyed by vandals in 1942, but cannot now recall the primary source. If the disc was destroyed then, it is odd that Parker did not mention this in the articles he wrote for *London & North Eastern Railway Magazine* in March 1943 or April 1946 (in these articles he mentions damage to the indicators at Blue Hill and Tinto Hill, which he also designed). As late as 1974, the *AA Illustrated Road Book* asserts in its entry on Ben Nevis that 'a mountain indicator gives particulars of the wide view that can be enjoyed.' At any rate, a reference in *Hamish's Mountain Walk* suggests the disc was gone by 1978. The

*J.A. Parker checks the orientation of the disc on the Ben Nevis indicator, 29 July 1927. Source: Gordon Wilson, SMCJ Vol. 18*

plinth remains. Both James E. Shearer and Chris Jesty have drawn panoramas from Ben Nevis.

James E. Shearer, *Panorama seen from the Observatory on the summit of Ben Nevis* (8 ft 1 inch x 5¼ inches). Stirling: R.S. Shearer and Son, 1895.

'Ben Nevis – unveiling ceremony', *The Scotsman*, 9 August 1927

J.A. Parker, 'Erecting of the Mountain Indicator on the Summit of Ben Nevis', *Scottish Mountaineering Club Journal*, Vol. 18, number 104, November 1927, pp.71–74 (includes diagram of design on the disc)

*AA Illustrated Road Book of Scotland*, 6th edition, 1974, p.114

Chris Jesty, *Ben Nevis Panorama* (2 ft 8¼ inches x 9¾ inches). Bridport: Jesty's Panoramas, 1977 (revised 1980)

Hamish Brown, *Hamish's Mountain Walk*, 1978, p.169

Ken Crocket, *Ben Nevis*, 1986, p.117

# NAIRNSHIRE

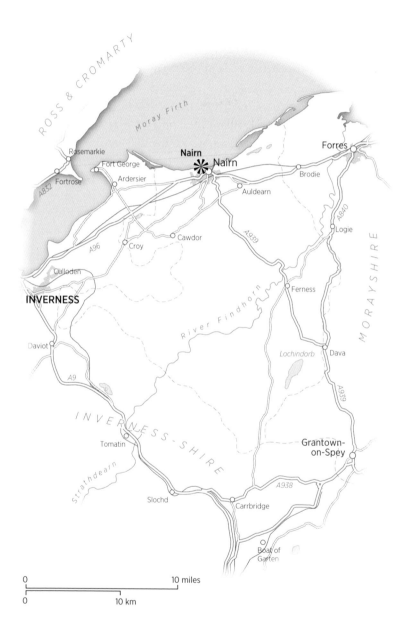

# Nairnshire

Nairn    ⚡                                             NH 878 570

Metal disc on a stone cairn. Designed by John Barker, erected by the Glasgow Nairnshire Association and unveiled on Sunday, 18 July 1954. Ben Macdhui is not visible.

'View Indicator is accepted for Nairn', *The Nairnshire Telegraph*, 20 July 1954.

# MORAY

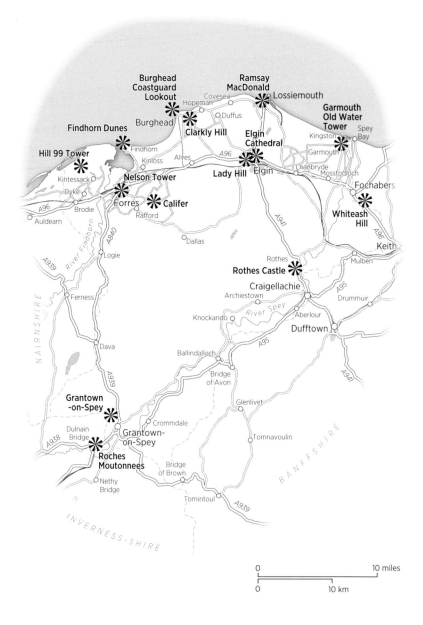

Findhorn Dunes
Hill 99 Tower
Nelson Tower
Forres
Califer
Burghead Coastguard Lookout
Burghead
Clarkly Hill
Ramsay MacDonald
Lossiemouth
Elgin Cathedral
Lady Hill
Garmouth Old Water Tower
Fochabers
Whiteash Hill
Keith
Rothes Castle
Craigellachie
Dufftown
Grantown-on-Spey
Roches Moutonnees

Covesea
Hopeman
Duffus
Findhorn
Kinloss
Alves
Kintessack
Dyke
Brodie
Auldearn
Rafford
Dallas
Logie
Ferness
Dava
Archiestown
Knockando
Ballindalloch
Bridge of Avon
Glenlivet
Crommdale
Dulnain Bridge
Grantown-on-Spey
Nethy Bridge
Bridge of Brown
Tomnavoulin
Tomintoul

Spey Bay
Kingston
Garmouth
Lhanbryde
Mosstodloch
Elgin
Mulben
Rothes
Aberlour
Drummuir

NAIRNSHIRE
BANFFSHIRE
INVERNESS-SHIRE

River Findhorn
River Spey

A96
A941
A95
A96
A940
A939
A938
A939
A941

0        10 miles
0        10 km

# MORAY

## Ramsay MacDonald
NJ 234 705

Panel with labelled photograph. Designed by the artist Suzie Tisch and erected by Lossiemouth Business Association in October 2010. The panel is mounted on the railings of a viewing platform on Prospect Terrace. The peak identified as Ben Aigan 471m is Knockan 372m; the peak identified as Ben Rinnes 840m is Brown Muir 339m.

'Lossie unveils its tribute to a proud son', *The Northern Scot*, 22 October 2010

## Burghead Coastguard Lookout
NJ 108 691

Square panel on a concrete cube. Designed by the graphic artist John Tasker of Drybridge near Buckie and erected by Burghead Headland Trust c.2001/02. The panel is sited on the top of a Coastguard Lookout Post, now converted into a visitor centre. Access is by means of a staircase. The peak identified as Hill of Oliclett is Ben-a-chielt (the Hill of Oliclett is below the sea horizon); the peak identified as Cairn Gorm must also be something else as Cairn Gorm is not visible.

Personal communication, Rhoda Davidson, Scottish Natural Heritage, 14 February 2011

## Clarkly Hill
NJ 127 683

Metal panel on a wooden frame. Designed by John Tasker and erected by Moray Council c.2000. The panel will be found a few yards from a fenced compound containing a reservoir.

Scottish Natural Heritage, *Facts and Figures*, 1999/2000, p.151
Response to FOI request, Moray Council, 4 November 2013

# Findhorn Dunes  NJ 041 648

Metal disc on a stone cylinder. Designed by Ron Philp and erected by Moray District Council in 1988. It stands on a circular concrete base surrounded by a stone wall. Four features are misidentified: the Hill of Oliclett 141m, Ben Rinnes 840m, Knock Hill 430m and the Monadhliath Mountains. None of these are visible.

'End in View for Dunes Project', *The Northern Scot*, 22 March 1988

'Viewpoint in from the Wilderness', *The Forres Gazette*, 22 June 1988

Countryside Commission for Scotland, *Twenty-First Report*, 1988, p. 61

*Findhorn Dunes. Photo taken 20/10/2012.*

# Garmouth Old Water Tower NJ 338 646

Metal disc on a stone cube. Erected by the Garmouth & Kingston Amenities Association in 1991. It will be found a few yards from a nineteenth century water tower (or Wr Twr as the Ordnance Survey *Explorer* has it). The Sutors of Cromarty, Tarbat Ness and Duncansby Head are not visible.

Countryside Commission for Scotland, *Twenty-Fourth Report*, 1991, p. 62

# Elgin Cathedral                                    NJ 221 630

Two panels mounted on one of the towers of a thirteenth century cathedral.
Erected by Historic Scotland in 2009. The viewing platform is on the north-west
tower. Access is by means of a door in the south-west tower and a mazy system
of walkways and spiral staircases. The cathedral is open throughout the year, but
there is an admission charge.

# Lady Hill                                          NJ 211 628

Bronze disc on a sandstone cylinder. Erected by the Elgin Fund in August 2010.
The indicator is about 25 yards from a nineteenth century stone column. Bin Hill
is not visible.

> 'Toposcope has town in view as landmark project unveiled', *The Northern Scot*, 3
> September 2010

# Hill 99 Tower                                      NH 986 623

Labelled outline of hills cut into the wooden railing of a viewing platform. The
viewing platform is at the top of a 20 metre tower and is reached by stairs. Built
by the Forestry Commission, the tower was opened to the public in June 2008.

> 'Forest Hits the Viewing Heights', *Forres Gazette*, 18 June 2008

# Nelson Tower                                       NJ 044 590

Plastic covered paper chart on a metal post. Designed by the trainee architect
Colette O'Sullivan, the chart was erected by the Rotary Club of Forres c.1985
and renewed in 2005. It is sited on top of an octagonal tower built in the
nineteenth century. The Nelson Tower chart was designed on the model of
Califer (see below) and inherits the eccentric spellings found on that indicator.
Am Faochagach 954m and Creag Ealraich 504m (spelt Carn Elric on the chart)
are not visible. The tower is currently open daily between two and four p.m. from
April to September.

> Personal communication, Alasdair Joyce, Falconer Museum

# Whiteash Hill                                      NJ 373 574

Framed paper chart on a stone plinth. Erected by the Forestry Commission c.2001. It will be found about ten yards from a nineteenth century stone pyramid commemorating the Duchess of Richmond.

Personal communication, Doug Collins, Forestry Commission, 11 February 2010

## Califer          NJ 084 570

Metal plate, 32 inches by 14 inches, mounted on a C-shaped stone wall. Designed by Hugh W. Cowper and erected by Moray District Council c.1985. Cowper was a maths teacher at Forres Academy. The spelling of some of the peaks is eccentric. For example, Creag Ealraich 504m is rendered as Carn Elric. Sgurr nan Conbhairean 1109m and Creag Ealraich 504m are not visible.

Countryside Commission for Scotland, *Fifteenth Report*, 1982, p. 41 and *Eighteenth Report*, 1985, p.41

*Califer. The plate gives directions for more than sixty landscape features. Photo taken 08/11/2013.*

## Rothes Castle         NJ 276 489

Square metal plate on a stone plinth. Moira Taylor tells me this indicator was erected by Moray Council c.2000. It is sited among the remains of a thirteenth century castle.

Personal communication, Moira Taylor, Moray Council, 7 January 2010

## Grantown-on-Spey 🌀      NJ 025 291

Framed paper chart on a stone cairn. Erected by J. Shanks of Barrhead, the manufacturer of sanitary ware, in 1914. The local committee which prepared the chart was assisted by A. Inkson McConnochie, one of the founders of the Cairngorm Club. When I visited on 19 May 2009, a paper copy of the original chart was on the cairn.

*Panoramic & Contour View of Grampian Range, from View Point, Grantown-on-Spey*, Aberdeen : London : G. Cornwall & Sons, 1914 (the chart)

'Contour View of the Cairngorms', *Cairngorm Club Journal*, Volume 8, issue 44, January 1915, p.82

## Roches Moutonnees 🌀      NJ 001 250

Metal plate on a stone plinth. Designed by Janet Munslow and erected by Highland Regional Council c.1980. Even when the plate was made, the view was partly obscured by trees, but each year that passes the field of view is narrowed. Four of the twenty peaks are misidentified.

Minutes of Highland Regional Council Leisure & Recreation Committee for 8 May 1980

Personal communication, Janet Munslow, 3 March 2010

# BANFFSHIRE

MORAYSHIRE

ABERDEENSHIRE

Cairngorms

Macduff
Banff
Gardenstown
Turriff
A98
A947
Portsoy
Aberchirder
A97
Cullen
Bin of Cullen
A95
A96
Portknockie
Findochty
Portessie
Buckie
Portgordon
Mosstodloch
Fochabers
Kirktown of Deskford
Gordonstown
Davoch of Grange
Keith
Huntly
Rhynie
Glenkindie
A941
A96
A920
A941
Drummuir
Bridgend
Cabrach
A97
A944
Rothes
Craigellachie
Aberlour
Dufftown
Ben Rinnes
A95
Bridge of Avon
Ballindalloch
Drumin
Crommdale
Glenlivet
Tomnavoulin
Cairn Daimh
Glenmulliach
Strathdon
Cock Bridge
A939
A944
Bridge of Brown
Tomintoul
Queen Victoria
Ben Avon
Grantown-on-Spey
A939
A938

10 miles
10 km

# BANFFSHIRE

## Macduff

NJ 701 643

Metal half-disc on a stone cube. Erected to commemorate the bicentenary of the burgh of Macduff in 1983. It is sited a few yards from the market cross opposite Macduff Parish Church, and is reached by stairs. All the peaks named on the plate are visible, although Morven and Scaraben, described as the 'Hills of Sutherland', are in Caithness. Orkney and Shetland are beyond the horizon.

## Bin of Cullen

NJ 479 642

Metal disc on a stone cylinder. Erected by the Rotary Club of Buckie to mark the Millennium, c.2006. There was previously a pill box at the site.

Record for Bin of Cullen on Trigpointinguk

## Ben Rinnes

NJ 255 354

Metal disc mounted on top of an Ordnance Survey triangulation pillar. Erected by the Directors of the Whisky Festival of Speyside, and unveiled on Sunday, 3 May 2009 in the presence of around thirty whisky enthusiasts.

Press release on the Friends of Ben Rinnes website (friendsofbenrinnes.org.uk).

## Carn Daimh

NJ 181 249

Metal disc on a stone cairn. Designed by the artist John Cannavan and erected by the Crown Estate in 1990; renewed 1997/98 and 2011. The disc photographed by Richard Webb carried a labelled outline of the hills on the horizon; the most recent version simply gives directions for the surrounding features.

'Viewpoint Indicator', photo taken in 2005 by Richard Webb on Geograph

Personal communications, Andrew Wells, the Crown Estate, 6 May 2009, John Cannavan, 19 October 2010 and Vicky Hilton, the Crown Estate, 30 September 2014.

# Glenmulliach

NJ 207 186

Plastic covered paper chart on a stone plinth. Designed by John Cannavan and erected by the Crown Estate in 1990. Three of the seven peaks are misidentified.

> Personal communications, Andrew Wells, the Crown Estate, 6 May 2009 and John Cannavan, 19 October 2010

*A chart at the Glenmulliach viewpoint depicts the rolling hills to the west. Photo taken 30/09/2009.*

# Queen Victoria 🏴 NJ 164 172

Metal plate on a stone plinth. Erected by Moray District Council c.1986. The peak identified as Big Garvoun 741m is Tom an Reisg 482m. The Big Garvoun is not visible.

Countryside Commission for Scotland, *Nineteenth Report*, 1986, p. 54

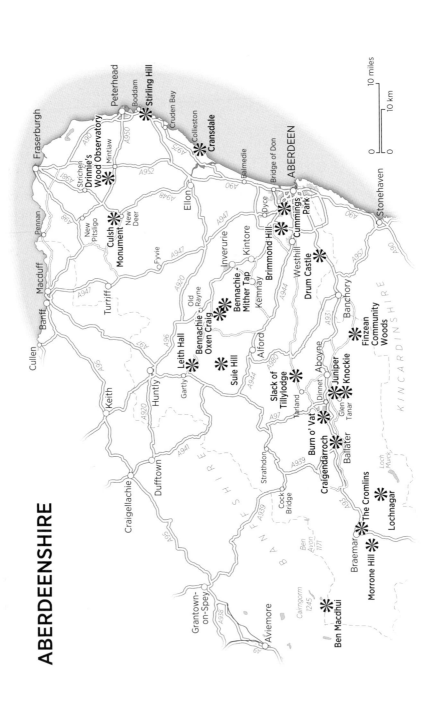

# ABERDEENSHIRE

Cullen
Banff
Macduff
Pennan
Fraserburgh
Peterhead
Boddam
**Stirling Hill**
Cruden Bay
Collieston
**Cransdale**
Balmedie
Bridge of Don
**ABERDEEN**
Stonehaven
Strichen
New Pitsligo
New Deer
Mintlaw
**Drinnie's Wood Observatory**
**Culsh Monument**
Fyvie
Turriff
Keith
Huntly
Gartly
Old Rayne
Inverurie
Kintore
Kemnay
Ellon
Dyce
Westhill
**Cummings Park**
**Brimmond Hill**
**Drum Castle**
Banchory
**Finzean Community Woods**
**Bennachie Mither Tap**
**Bennachie Oxen Craig**
**Leith Hall**
**Suie Hill**
Alford
**Slack of Tillylodge**
Tarland
Aboyne
Dinnet
**Juniper Knockie**
Glen Tanar
**Burn o' Vat**
**Craigendarroch**
**Ballater**
Strathdon
Cock Bridge
**The Cromlins**
**Lochnagar**
Loch Muick
Braemar
**Morrone Hill**
Dufftown
Craigellachie
Grantown-on-Spey
Aviemore
Cairngorm 1245
Ben Avon 1171
Ben Macdhui
**Ben Macdhui**

KINCARDINSHIRE
BANFFSHIRE

10 miles
10 km
0

# Aberdeenshire

## Drinnie's Wood Observatory

NJ 973 498

Four framed paper charts, one for each point of the compass. They were installed by Banff and Buchan District Council in 1993. The charts are sited in the upper storey of an octagonal tower built in the nineteenth century. Access is by means of a spiral staircase inside the tower. The peak identified as Lochnagar is Morven 871m. Lochnagar is hidden by Bennachie.

## Culsh Monument

NJ 881 483

Panels set on a granite plinth. Designed by the Scottish Sculpture Workshop, erected by Banff & Buchan District Council and unveiled on Wednesday, 11 September 1991. The granite slabs of the plinth were originally part of the grand Cruden Bay Hotel, which was demolished in the fifties, and were then used for an extension to a school in Peterhead. When that too was demolished they were used to make this plinth. The panels are reached by three steps.

'Monument to first MP reopened', *Press and Journal*, 12 September 1991

Countryside Commission for Scotland, *Twenty Fourth Report*, 1991–92, p.62

Personal communication, Hamish Robertson, Aberdeenshire Council, 5 January 2011

## Stirling Hill

NK 122 409

Metal disc on a stone cylinder. Erected by Boddam Community Association in 2012.

## Leith Hall

NJ 542 303

Metal plate set on the south-facing wall of a square stone enclosure. Erected by the National Trust for Scotland in June 1981. The plate carries a labelled photograph.

*A labelled photograph interprets the view at Leith Hall. Photo taken 21/05/2009.*

## Cransdale 🌀                         NK 042 285

Panel on a stone plinth. Erected by Gordon District Council in the late 1980s.

> Personal communication, Andrews Carruthers, Aberdeenshire Council, 28
> January 2010

## Suie Hill 🌀                          NJ 546 233

There are two panels at this site, both erected by Gordon District Council. One is dated 1981 and is mounted on metal posts. The other is dated 1990 and was originally mounted on wooden posts. Both carry labelled drawings of the view north-west. When I visited on 20 May 2009, the 1990 panel was lying damaged on the ground.

## Bennachie – Mither Tap 🌀              NJ 682 223

Copper disc, protected by glass, on a stone cylinder. Designed by James Mackay, erected by the Bailies of Bennachie, and unveiled on 14 or 15 July 1974. The copper disc was replaced by a stainless steel one in 1980. There is some footage of both of the indicators on Bennachie in a film produced by the Bailies called *A Postcard from Bennachie.*

'Inverurie boys' Bennachie indicator unveiled', *Press & Journal*, 15 July 1974

Archie Whiteley (ed.), *The Book of Bennachie*, 1976, plates between pp.66 and 67

Personal communication, James Mackay, 26 April 2009

*Summit of the Mither Tap of Bennachie. Both of the main tops of Bennachie have view indicators. Photo taken 08/12/2009.*

# Bennachie – Oxen Craig 🏴 NJ 662 225

Stainless steel disc on a stone cylinder. Designed by James Mackay, erected by the Bailies of Bennachie and unveiled on Saturday, 14 October 1989.

> *Press & Journal*, 16 October 1989
>
> Countryside Commission for Scotland, *Twenty Second Report*, 1989, p. 59
>
> Personal communication, James Mackay, 26 April 2009

# Brimmond Hill 🏴 NJ 856 091

Square brass plate on a metal post. Designed by G. Gordon Jenkins, with assistance from James A. Parker. Erected by the Stoneywood Literary Guild and unveiled on Saturday, 2 June 1917. The plate is protected by a removable cover. A folding panorama of the view from the summit of Brimmond Hill drawn by Alexander Copland had been published more than twenty years earlier.

> Alexander Copland, *The Brimmond Hill* (23½ inches x 22½ inches). *Cairngorm Club Journal*, Volume 1, issue 4, January 1895.
>
> 'Brimmond Hill: Index Chart & War Memorial', *Aberdeen Free Press*, 4 June 1917
>
> 'Brimmond Hill War Memorial', *Aberdeen Daily Journal*, 4 June 1917
>
> 'War Memorials', *Aberdeen Daily Journal*, 4 June 1917
>
> James Cruickshank, 'Mountain Indicator on Brimmond', *Cairngorm Club Journal*, Volume 9, issue 49, July 1917, pp.1–7

# Cummings Park NJ 909 082

Stainless steel disc on a stone cylinder. Four carved stone benches mark the points of the compass. Erected by Aberdeen City Council and unveiled on Wednesday, 11 September 2013. Digital models suggest that Elrick Hill is hidden by Brimmond Hill.

> 'Compass stones take a seat in the right direction', Aberdeen City Council press release, 11 September 2013.

# Slack of Tillylodge 🏴 NJ 523 061

Metal disc on a stone cylinder. Erected by the Deeside Field Club and unveiled on Saturday, 12 September 1970. Corse Hill and Mortlich are not visible.

'Slack of Tillylodge indicator marks Deeside Field Club 50th anniversary', *Press & Journal*, 14 September 1970 (photo of unveiling)

'Excursions and Activities of the Deeside Field Club 1970–1973', *The Deeside Field* 3rd series, No.1, 1974

## Drum Castle                                                    NJ 792 001

Panel on wooden legs. Erected by the National Trust for Scotland in 2004.

Personal communication, Fiona Milne, NTS

## Burn O'Vat                                                     NO 428 997

Three wooden panels mounted on a wooden viewing platform. Installed by Scottish Natural Heritage in April 2012.

'New horizons at Muir of Dinnet', SNH press release, 12 April 2012

## Ben Macdhui                                                    NN 988 989

Doulton stoneware disc on a granite cylinder. Designed by James A. Parker, erected by the Cairngorm Club and unveiled on Saturday, 1 August 1925. A notebook was carried around those present at the unveiling ceremony by a Boy Scout, who collected 136 signatures. Ben Cleuch appears to the west of the high point of Ben a'Ghlo, rather than the east, as the disc suggests. Alexander Copland had previously published a folding panorama drawn from Ben Macdhui.

*A contemporary postcard of the indicator on Ben Macdhui.*

Alexander Copland, *The Horizon from Ben Muich Dhui* (17 ft 8 inches x 4½ inches), published in four sections in the *Cairngorm Club Journal*, Volumes 2 and 3, 1897–1900

Robert Clarke, 'Inauguration of the Ben Macdhui Indicator', *Cairngorm Club Journal*, Volume 11, issue 64, July 1926, pp.185–190

James A. Parker, 'Erecting the Indicator: Diary of the Building Operations', *Cairngorm Club Journal*, Volume 11, issue 64, July 1926, pp.191–197

'Mountain Indicator on Scottish Peak', *The Times*, 28 July 1925

'Ben Macdhui Indicator', *The Scotsman*, 29 July 1925

## Juniper 🔆                                    NO 480 967

Framed paper chart on wooden legs. Erected by the Glen Tanar Charitable Trust, c.2008.

Personal communication, Eric Baird, Glen Tanar Ranger Service, 4 May 2009

## Craigendarroch 🔆                             NO 365 965

Bronze disc on a stone cylinder. Erected by Ballater Royal Deeside Ltd in 2003. Contrary to the statement on the disc, not all the hills whose directions are given can be seen in clear weather. Broad Cairn 998m and Peter's Hill 568m are both hidden by closer ground.

Cairngorm Local Action Group website, cairngorms-leader.org

## Knockie 🔆            NO 479 952

Laminated panel on wooden legs. Designed by Brian Hart and erected by the Glen Tanar Charitable Trust, c.1987. The peak identified as Tom Giubhais 417m is Monrae. Tom Giubhais is not visible.

Countryside Commission for Scotland, *Twenty Second Report*, 1989, p. 59

Personal communication, Eric Baird, Glen Tanar Ranger Service, 4 May 2009

*Craigendarroch, above Ballater, on a winter day. Photo taken 14/02/2010.*

## Finzean Community Woods                       NO 615 924

Laminated panel on a stone cube. Erected by the Birse Community Trust c.2001 to mark the Millennium.

Personal communication, Robin Callander, Birse Community Trust, 5 January 2011

*A panel installed at Finzean Community Woods looks West to the Forest of Birse. Photo taken 05/01/2011.*

## The Cromlins <NO 156 919>

Framed paper chart on metal legs. Erected by the Braemar Civic Amenities Trust, c.1988. The arrow for Ben Avon points to part of the nearer peak of Creag a'Chleirich. (A small portion of Ben Avon can be seen between Creag a'Chleirich and the conifer plantation immediately north of the chart.)

> Personal communication, Bill Marshall, Braemer Civic Amenities Trust, 15 January 2010

## Morrone Hill <NO 142 905>

Bronze disc on a synthetic granite pillar. Designed by the architect Fenton Wyness with the assistance of Hugh D. Welsh of the Cairngorm Club, erected by the Deeside Field Club and unveiled on Saturday, 3 September 1960. It marked the Field Club's fortieth anniversary. The original synthetic granite pillar has been replaced by a stone cylinder.

The Scottish Mountaineering Club guidebook to the Corbetts suggests that originally it was intended to site the indicator on a knoll which is about 80m south of the indicator, and 17m higher: 'Originally it was intended to site [the indicator] 17m higher, and not all the points shown on it are visible from its present position.'

It is doubtful that the indicator was misplaced. Architectural drawings by Fenton Wyness in the archive of the Deeside Field Club include a site plan for the device which corresponds closely to its current location. Moreover, a portion of all 24 peaks on the disc can be seen, although their summits are hidden in some cases. However, there is one positional error: the direction given for Ben Avon is incorrect (it should be between Carn na Drochaide and Creag a'Chleirich).

Hugh D. Welsh and Fenton Wyness, *The Morrone Hill Indicator*, 1960, booklet published by The Deeside Field Club

'Cairngorm Guide on Braemar Hilltop', *Press & Journal*, 5 September 1960

'Hill Indicator at Braemar', *Deeside Field*, 2nd Series, No. 4, 1962, p.69

Architectural plan by Fenton Wyness in the Deeside Field Club Archive.

'The Deeside Field Club's View Indicator on Morrone', photo by Colin Smith on Geograph (shows the original pillar)

SMC guide, *The Corbetts*, 1990, p.93

# Lochnagar                                                        NO 243 861

Doulton stoneware disc on a granite cylinder. Designed by James A. Parker, erected by the Cairngorm Club and unveiled on Saturday, 12 July 1924. According to the list made of those present, 143 people attended the ceremony, which concluded with a rendition of 'God Save the King'.

'The View from Lochnagar: Mountain Indicator Unveiled', *The Scotsman*, 14 July 1924

Henry Alexander, 'The Lochnagar Indicator: Its Building and Unveiling', *Cairngorm Club Journal*, Volume 11, issue 62, September 1924, pp.53–67

'The King's Interest', *The Scotsman*, 16 December 1924

*A postcard published by J. & J. Bissett photographers,*
*Ballater, of the indicator on the summit of Lochnagar.*

# KINCARDINESHIRE

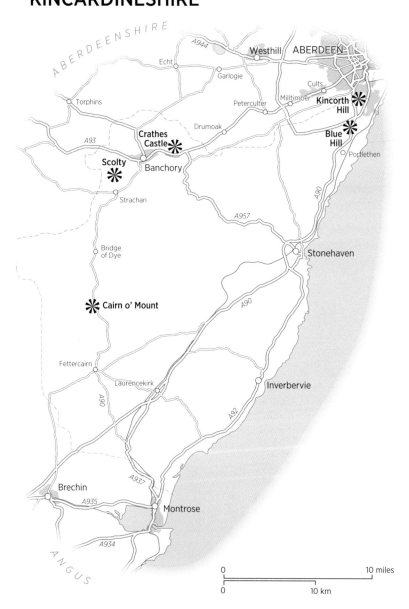

ABERDEENSHIRE

A944

Echt

Westhill    ABERDEEN

Garlogie

Cults

Torphins

Peterculter    Milltimber    Kincorth
Hill

Drumoak

Crathes
Castle    Blue
Hill

A93

Scolty    Banchory    Portlethen

Strachan

A957

Bridge
of Dye

Stonehaven

Cairn o' Mount

A90

Fettercairn

A90    Laurencekirk    Inverbervie

A92

Brechin    A937

A935    Montrose

A934

ANGUS

0                                    10 miles

0                            10 km

# KINCARDINESHIRE

## Kincorth Hill
NJ 937 026

Plastic covered paper chart, about 6 feet long and 1 foot wide, on a stone plinth. Erected by Aberdeen City Council in the summer of 2001. Five of the seven peaks are misidentified.

> Personal communication, Grant Webster, Aberdeen City Council, 8 January 2013

## Blue Hill
NJ 924 003

Doulton stoneware disc on a granite cylinder. Designed by James A. Parker, erected by the Cairngorm Club and unveiled on Saturday, 2 November 1929. A panorama from Blue Hill drawn by A. Cruickshank and A. Copland had appeared more than thirty years earlier. Some of the identifications were criticised by the engineer G. Gordon Jenkins who published a proposed design for an indicator in *Hill Views of Aberdeen*. Parker's 1929 design was a simplification of this. The indicator was vandalised in November 1942, about half the disc being broken away, but remnants survived until the mid-1980s. A metal replacement was installed on the plinth by North Kincardine Rural Community Council in 1997. The design of the new disc (due to W. Anderson of Banchory) stays closer to G. Gordon Jenkins' original proposal than did Parker. Strathfinella Hill is not visible.

> Alexander Cruickshank and Alexander Copland, 'The Blue Hill', *Cairngorm Club Journal*, Volume 1, issue 1, July 1893, pp. 29–45 (the folding panorama, 23" by 19", is titled 'View from the Blue Hill of Mountains, Hills, &c in the Horizon and foreground in Outline')
>
> G. Gordon Jenkins, *Hill Views of Aberdeen*, 1917
>
> 'Blue Hill Indicator', *Aberdeen Journal*, 4 November 1929 (pictures taken at the unveiling ceremony)
>
> 'Blue Hill Indicator: The Unveiling Ceremony', *Cairngorm Club Journal*, Volume 12, issue 69, January 1930, pp.122–129
>
> 'Blue Hill Vandalism', *Aberdeen Journal*, 25 November 1942 (picture of smashed disc)

James A. Parker, 'The British Mountains over Three Thousand Feet', *London & North-Eastern Railway Magazine*, vol.33, no.3, March 1943, pp.42–43

James A. Parker, 'View Indicators on Mountains', *London & North-Eastern Railway Magazine*, vol.36, Number 4, April 1946, pp.80–81

Record for Blue Hill: Cairn on RCAHMS database (Canmore ID 20253) in particular Item A35437, a photograph of the indicator taken in 1983

Dave Hewitt, 'Engineering a way up the hills 1000 times over', *The Scotsman*, 7 August 1999

# Crathes Castle                                                   NO 731 967

Panel on a wooden frame. Erected by the National Trust for Scotland in 1990. Since then the panel has been renewed twice, most recently in 2003.

Personal communication, Fiona Milne, NTS

# Scolty                                                          NO 678 939

Two bronze discs, mounted on granite pillars about 20 yards apart. The indicators were installed by the Rotary Club of Banchory as part of a refurbishment of the nearby nineteenth century tower. The refurbished tower was opened by Prince Charles on Tuesday, 15 September 1992. More than 100 people attended the ceremony, which was conducted in notably windy conditions.

Cuidhe Crom 1083m is hidden behind the Gathering Cairn 790m, a peak in the Mount Keen group. Confusingly, some of the spellings of the hills are not consistent with Ordnance Survey maps.

'Charles wins hearts on windy Scolty', *Deeside Piper*, 18 September 1992

Countryside Commission for Scotland, *Twenty Fourth Report*, 1991/92, p.63

Personal communication, Phil Taylor, Rotary Club of Banchory

# Cairn o'Mount                                                   NO 650 804

Panel on metal legs adjacent to a wall. Andrew Carruthers told me that folk memory suggests the panel was installed by Kincardine & Deeside District Council around 1990.

Personal communication, Andrew Carruthers, Aberdeeenshire Council, 21 May 2009

*One of the two bronze discs mounted at the summit of Scolty by the Rotary Club of Banchory. Photo taken 02/07/2009.*

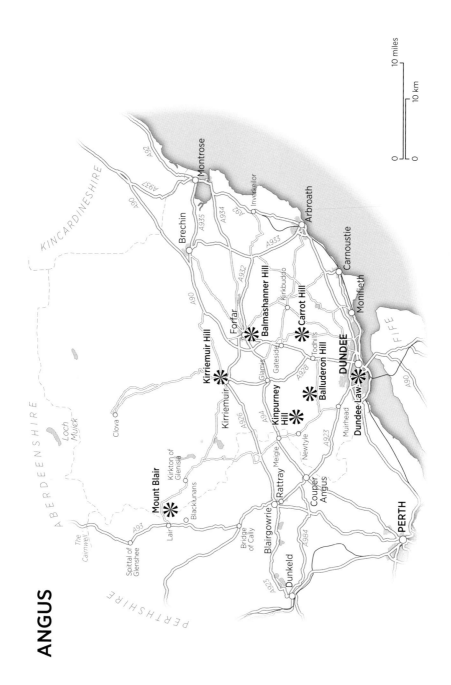

ANGUS

# Angus

## Mount Blair

NO 167 629

Metal strip mounted on a circular stone wall. Designed by the artist Mary McGregor and dated 2003. A text box on the metal strip states: 'This viewpoint indicator was planned and commissioned by James G.S. Gammell of Forter before he died. It has been erected by his family and the National Trust for Scotland.' Mr. Gammell was also responsible for the nearby telecommunications mast (September 1999) and the access track leading to it. The National Trust for Scotland could not find any record of having provided assistance in the installation of the viewpoint indicator. The device was renewed in the summer of 2013.

Dave Hewitt, 'Mounting pressure for a mast protest', *The Scotsman*, 9 October 1999

Personal communication, Ian Riches, NTS, 26 February 2010

Walkhighlands website, records for Mount Blair.

## Kirriemuir Hill

NO 388 546

Bronze disc on a stone cylinder, sited on the verandah of a sports pavilion. Both the indicator and the pavilion were designed by the architect Frank Thomson of Dundee. They were gifted to Kirriemuir Town Council by J.M. Barrie (of *Peter Pan* fame) who was brought up in the town. The pavilion was formally opened by Barrie on Saturday, 7 June 1930 amid great publicity. Surviving Pathé newsreel footage of the opening ceremony includes part of Barrie's speech.

*The indicator at the pavilion on Kirriemuir Hill, gifted to the town by J.M. Barrie. Photo taken 22/08/2009.*

*The summit of Mount Blair. Since this photo was taken (15/02/2010), the indicator has been renewed.*

Access to the indicator is free, but if you want to gain an extra few metres of height, you can visit the camera obscura inside the pavilion, for which there is an admission charge. A leaflet published by Angus Council provides a description of the 'Commanding Views' based on the assumption that everything on the disc is visible. However, Carn Mairg, Ben Lui and Capel Mount are not visible (even with the aid of the camera obscura).

*Kirriemuir Free Press*, 12 June 1930 (pictures of opening ceremony)

Note and collection of press cuttings about the pavilion donated by Trixie Thomson (Frank Thomson's daughter) to Kirriemuir library.

'Thrums Revisited', Pathé newsreel issued 12 June 1930, Film ID 715.01

*Camera obscura and Kirriemuir*, leaflet available on the Angus Council website

# Balmashanner Hill                                    NO 455 492

Paper chart in a glass frame, with protecting meshed netting, mounted on a metal frame. Designed by John S. Ramsay and erected by Forfar Town Council around 25 June 1909. After ten years, the chart was reported to have been destroyed. Today all that remains of the original structure is the metal frame on which the chart stood, which has four legs and is painted green. This frame will be found about 30 yards west of a mobile phone mast.

In 1921 a War Memorial was unveiled on Balmashanner in the form of a 55 foot high stone look-out tower. By 1927, a copy of Ramsay's chart had been placed at the top of the tower, and there appears to have been a copy of the chart here as late as 1986, when it was mentioned by Ernest S. Mann. But there was no chart at the top of the tower when I visited on 17 March 2011 (the tower is normally locked; to discuss access contact Angus Council).

The view indicator which stands today on Balmshanner Hill was unveiled on Thursday, 5 September 1929. It consists of a gun-metal half disc on a metal post, and is located at grid reference NO 459 494, about 500 yards from where the 1909 chart stood. The design of the plate is a near copy of that chart, although it omits some notes about the hills (including a geological note) and also the name of the designer. It was unveiled on the same day as the nearby pavilion, or shelter, which was a gift to Forfar Town Council by the businessman James Anderson, a native of the town. Anderson's gift was inspired by the pavilion that had been given to Kirriemuir by J.M. Barrie (see above).

In May 2010, a letter in the *Forfar Despatch* complained that around a quarter of the mountains named on the indicator were no longer visible owing to the height to which the surrounding trees had been allowed to grow. The peak identified as Driesh is Mayar.

John S. Ramsay (1879–1927) worked first in the Post Office at Forfar, and then Kirkcaldy. In 1923, he published a panorama drawn from Falkland Hill (East Lomond). A reviewer in the *Cairngorm Club Journal* wrote: 'Mr. Ramsay, we understand, has been studying for quarter of a century mountain views seen from Central Scotland, and has constructed many charts for his own pleasure. A number of these charts were exhibited for several months in the rooms in Edinburgh of the Royal Geographical Society'. In a similar vein, in his 1927 guidebook *Highways and Byways of Strathmore*, Ramsay wrote: 'hill views are described, not from memory merely, but from careful drawings made throughout a period of over a quarter of a century.' As far as I am aware, the surviving examples of Ramsay's work are the Balmashanner indicator, the Falkland Hill panorama, and the outline drawings of the views from Kinpurney Hill and the Knockie, near Blairgowrie, in *Highways and Byways*. An article in the *Evening Telegraph* refers to a chart he prepared of the Grampian peaks to be seen from Kinpurnie Castle around 1911 for the benefit of its proprietor Sir Charles Kayzer.

'The view from "Bummy"', letter from 'Onlooker', *Forfar Herald*, 17 May 1907

'Chart of Mountains', *Forfar Herald*, 26 February 1909

*Forfar Herald*, 25 June 1909 (reports erection of chart)

'Forfar War Memorial', *Forfar Review*, 26 December 1919 (chart reported destroyed)

John S. Ramsay, *Mountains, etc, seen from Balmashanner, Forfar* (I am grateful to A.B. Whyte of Forfar for sending me a copy of Ramsay's paper chart of 1909)

'Falkland Hill Panorama', *Cairngorm Club Journal*, Volume 11, issue 61, p.47, July 1923

John S. Ramsay, *Highways and Byways of Strathmore and the Northern Glens*, 1927, p.11–12

'At the Top of Kinpurnie', *Evening Telegraph*, 20 June 1927

Obituary of John S. Ramsay in the *Forfar Herald*, 4 November 1927

'Freedom of the Burgh: Mrs Anderson Opens New Pavilion at Balmashanner', *Forfar Herald*, 6 September 1929

R.W. Dill, *Beauty Spots in and around Forfar*, 1930, p79–85

Ernest S. Mann, *A Historical Walk Around Bummie*, 1986, 24-page pamphlet

'Can't see the View for the Trees!', *Forfar Despatch*, 19 May 2010

# Kinpurney Hill        NO 322 417

Metal disc on a stone cylinder. Designed by Pat Roberton and Grant Innes and erected by the Newtyle Path Network in 2004. The peaks identified as Ben More 1174m, Carn Gorm 1029m, Lochnagar 1155m and Mount Keen 939m are all other objects. With the exception of part of the shoulder of Carn Gorm, none of these are visible. The mistakes on the indicator are repeated in the booklet below. John S. Ramsay published a description of the view from the Kinpurney Hill, including an outline drawing, in the 1920s.

John S. Ramsay, *Highways and Byways of Strathmore and the Northern Glens*, 1927 (pp. 10–11, illustration facing page 8)

*The Den and Kinpurney Hill, Newtyle Path Network*, booklet published by John Blackburn Buick in 2005 (available in Newtyle Post Office)

## Carrot Hill NO 463 408

Metal plate on a stone plinth. Designed by Blue Square Design (Dundee) and erected by Inverarity Community Council in 2001 to mark the Millennium. The peak identified as Glas Maol is Glas Tulaichean; the peak identified as Lochnagar is Driesh.

Personal communication, Roy Madden, Angus Council, 8 January 2010

## Balluderon Hill NO 361 394

Metal disc on a stone cairn, topped with a block of Aberdeenshire granite. A tribute to the blind climber Syd Scroggie (1919–2006), it was unveiled on Tuesday, 27 June 2000 in his presence.

'Hill cairn tribute to the courage of Syd Scroggie', *The Courier and Advertiser*, 28 June 2000 (picture of Scroggie at the cairn)

*Balluderon Hill. Photo taken 27/12/2009.*

## Dundee Law NO 391 313

Bronze disc on a fluted metal post. Designed by the architect Alexander Hutcheson, assisted by John W. Lowdon, and erected by the Town Council of Dundee in August 1900. The device, described as a Geographical Compass, was proposed by David Mathers, Convener of the Recreation and Cemeteries Committee of the council.

In February 1936, a correspondent in *The Courier and Advertiser* drew attention to the condition of the indicator (the paper reported that 'in some cases the names have become barely legible'). They also raised doubt as to whether it is possible

*The Geographical Compass at the summit of Dundee Law. Photo taken 07/03/2010.*

to see Ben Macdhui and Ben Doran. Lowdon defended the indicator, explaining that he and Hutcheson had worked out what could be seen using string and maps laid out on the floor of Hutcheson's room. They had then taken a theodolite to the top of Law and identified all the peaks; seeing Ben Macdhui took more than a week owing to bad visibility, and Ben Doran was a similar case. 'We were very careful in our calculations to see that no mistake was made', he explained.

At the start of the Second World War, the disc was removed by the authorities on the grounds that in the event of a German invasion it 'might be of assistance to the enemy'. It was restored in November 1944.

In December 1944, Dr George Miller re-opened the question of the accuracy of the indicator, saying that he had 'applied the formula of J.A. Parker' and that, contrary to the assurance given by Lowdon, Ben Macdhui and Ben Doran were not visible. Parker confirmed this, telling Miller that some years ago he had studied the matter on the ground by climbing to the gap to the immediate east of Kinpurnie Hill, which is on the line of sight between Dundee Law and Ben Macdhui.

Digital models of the view suggest Miller and Parker were correct. Despite this, the claim that Macdhui is visible has continued to appear in newspaper articles, educational works directed at schoolchildren and tourist guidebooks.

In 1974, the disc was stolen. Twenty years later, it was anonymously left in the garden of a Dundee resident and re-attached to the plinth. Apart from Ben Macdhui and Ben Doran, Kinnoull Hill is also hidden.

Minutes of the Recreation and Cemeteries Committee, Dundee Town Council, 18 December 1899 and 15 January, 18 June and 14 November 1900

Alexander Elliot, 'Dundee Law', *Cairngorm Club Journal*, Volume 3, number 17, July 1901, pp.303–309

'Does the Law Indicator Fib?', *The Courier and Advertiser*, 22 February 1936

'The Law Gets its Indicator', *The Courier and Advertiser*, 14 November 1944

'The Law's Fib?', *The Courier and Advertiser*, 7 December 1944

'High Life Indeed!', *The Courier and Advertiser*, 19 May 1949 (includes reproduction of disc, which shows the direction of forty-one objects)

Nancy Davey, *Urban Studies in Dundee*, 1978, p.5

Michelin Guide, *Scotland*, 1st edition, 1985, p.76

'Law viewfinder back on plinth', *The Courier and Advertiser*, 10 December 1994

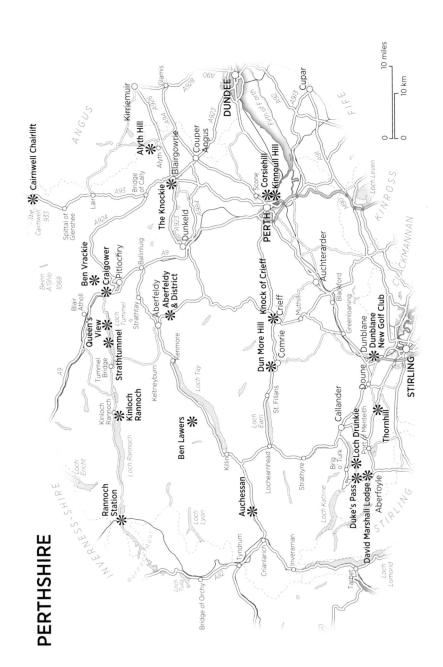

# Perthshire

## Cairnwell Chairlift                                NO 134 775

A vertical wooden post, on which were attached signs pointing to surrounding peaks. The wooden post was mounted on a cairn, close to the upper terminus of the Cairnwell Chairlift. It seems most likely to have been installed by the Glenshee Chairlift Company around 1962, when the chairlift opened. It has since been removed. Current Ordnance Survey maps have a viewpoint symbol at the summit of Cairnwell, about two hundred metres from where the indicator stood.

> J. Arthur Dixon postcard titled 'Mountain Indicator and Chairlift, Glenshee, Perthshire'


## Ben Vrackie                                NN 950 631

Bronze disc on a stone cairn. The indicator commemorates the residence of the Leys School, Cambridge in Pitlochry during the Second World War. Designed by its headmaster, Dr W.G. Humphrey, the indicator was the gift of the masters and boys of the School to Pitlochry Town Council. It was unveiled on Saturday, 17 September 1949 in a ceremony attended by eighty people. The artist A. Scott Rankin published a panorama drawn from Ben Vrackie in the 1920s.

> A. Scott Rankin, *Seen from the top of Ben-y-Vrackie.* Pitlochry: L. Mackay, c.1923. (reviewed caustically in *Cairngorm Club Journal*, Volume 10, number 60, January 1923, pp.273–274)
>
> 'Indicator on Ben-y-Vrackie', *Perthshire Advertiser*, 7 September 1949
>
> 'Memorial Unveiled on Summit of Perthshire Ben', *Perthshire Advertiser*, 21 September 1949

## Craigower

NN 926 604

Framed paper chart on a stone plinth. Erected by the National Trust for Scotland in 1984, and renewed in 2005. The current chart, designed by Andy Milne, carries a labelled photograph.

Personal communication, Ben Notley, NTS, 4 March 2011

## Strathtummel

NN 818 601

Caithness stone slab on a stone cube. Erected by the Forestry Commission c.1996/97.

Personal communication, Peter Fullerton, Forestry Commission, 29 May 2009

## Queen's View

NN 863 597

Bronze plate on a stone plinth. Erected by the Automobile Association and unveiled on Wednesday, 17 July 1957. The Forestry Commission completely remodelled this site in 1995, creating a paved area with railings, and replacing the AA indicator with one in a very different style. This consists of a Caithness stone slab on a knee-high plinth.

'Guide to Tourists at Beauty Spot Queen Victoria Loved', *Perthshire Advertiser*, 20 July 1957

'Face Lift for Queen's View', *Perthshire Advertiser*, 10 March 1995

Personal communication, Peter Fullerton, Forestry Commission, 29 May 2009

## Kinloch Rannoch

NN 659 578

Laminated panel on a stone plinth. Erected in 1990 by Perth & Kinross District Council. Beinn a'Chrulaiste 857m and Ben Alder 1148m are misidentified. Neither is visible.

'£20,000 facelift for Kinloch Rannoch', *Perthshire Advertiser*, 15 December 1989

Countryside Commission for Scotland, *Twenty Third Report*, 1990, p.39

## Rannoch Station

NN 422 577

Laminated disc on a stone cairn. A metal finger-post is mounted in the centre of the cairn. Installed by Perth and Kinross Heritage Trust in 1999. Extended study of the disc is facilitated by a visit outside the midge season.

'£88,000 Rannoch Station upgrade', *Perthshire Advertiser*, 22 June 1999

*A laminated disc at Rannoch Station identifies the surrounding peaks. Photo taken 16/06/2009.*

# Alyth Hill                    NO 243 503

Stone table designed to be used in conjunction with a circular chart published in the *Burgh of Alyth Guide Book*. The chart, which gave the directions of more than forty landscape features, was drawn by Mr T.G. Philip MA., formerly on the teaching staff at Alyth Public School. The stone table was erected by Alyth Town Council around 9 June 1938.

Ian Anderson recalls that a brass disc showing surrounding features was installed on the table in the 1950s or 60s. This is presumably what is referred to in the *Shell Guide to Scotland* for 1965, which says that 'An indicator on the summit of the Hill of Alyth gives points that can be viewed to the S.'

By the 1990s, the disc was missing and the table had fallen into disrepair. In May 2010, the table was rebuilt by the Alyth Hill User Group and a copy of

T.G. Philip's circular chart, covered in plastic, attached to it. At the same time, the group installed a brass plaque on the side of the plinth with the words: 'The Commonty of Alyth Hill, owned for at least 600 years and for all time by the people of Alyth'.

Ownership of Alyth Hill is disputed, and the renovation of the indicator became an unlikely flash point. In August 2010, the Forestry Commission wrenched the brass plaque from the plinth, saying that the wording 'did not recognise the Commission's ownership.' However, a replacement was installed by locals the following month. Both the circular chart and the controversial plaque were there when I visited on 15 December 2012.

Alyth Town Council minutes, 12 April 1938 (table commissioned)

'Alyth's Mountain Indicator', *Alyth Gazette and Guardian,* 9 June 1938

*Burgh of Alyth Guide Book,* compiled by A.K. Lunan, 56 pages, not dated [c.1938]

Moray McLaren, *Shell Guide to Scotland,* 1965, p.74

'Battle lines drawn in Alyth Hill commonty dispute', *The Courier,* 6 September 2010

'Alyth Hill Commonty protestors strike back', *The Courier,* 20 September 2010

Ian Anderson, Alyth, personal communication, 6 January 2013

# Aberfeldy & District    NN 879 463

Laminated panel on a stone cube. Erected by the Rotary Club of Aberfeldy in 1985. Since the panel was installed, the view of the hills north of the A9 has been obscured by conifer plantations. Three of the ten peaks are misidentified.

# The Knockie    NO 164 458

Bronze disc on a flat-topped boulder. Designed by W.D.M. Falconer and J. D. Petrie and erected by Blairgowrie and Rattray Town Council around 9 June 1922. Ben Vrackie is not visible. The boulder was gifted by the farmer David Robertson who lived at the nearby house of East Gormack until his suicide in 1928.

A description of the view from the Knockie, including an outline drawing, appears in John S. Ramsay's guidebook.

'Blairgowrie as Holiday Resort', *Blairgowrie Advertiser*, 2 June 1922

'Helpful to Visitors', *Blairgowrie Advertiser*, 9 June 1922

John S. Ramsay, *Highways and Byways of Strathmore and the Northern Glens,* 1927 (pp.6–7, pp.14–15, and illustration facing page 10)

*Summit of the Knockie, Blairgowrie. Photo taken 22/08/2009.*

# Ben Lawers                                                          NN 636 414

Bronze disc on a stone cairn. Erected by the National Trust for Scotland and unveiled by Tom Weir on Saturday, 7 July 1956. By 1979, the bronze disc had been damaged and was removed. A new disc, which was in a laminated plastic material and carried the date 1980, was installed on 25 May 1981. This was also damaged, and it was removed by the Trust in September 1982. Since then, the plinth has been empty. The removal of the disc is reflected on Ordnance Survey maps: some old OS maps have a viewpoint symbol at the summit of Ben Lawers, but current editions do not. The replacement disc is currently stored in the Scottish Mountain Heritage Collection, an archive maintained by Mick Tighe of Roy Bridge. Images of it can be seen on the Collection's website.

'Unveiling Ceremony on County's Highest Peak', *Perthshire Advertiser*, 7 July 1956

Tom Weir, 'My Month' *The Scots Magazine*, September 1956, p.445

Personal communications, Helen Cole, NTS, 2 May 2009 and 25 Mar 2010 (I am grateful to Helen Cole for supplying images of the disc)

Personal communication, Ian Riches, NTS, 6 May 2009

Personal communication, Mick Tighe, 25 March 2013

*Tom Weir unveils the view indicator at the summit of
Ben Lawers. Source: National Trust for Scotland.*

## Auchessan                                          NN 446 276

When I visited this site on 8 January 1999 there was an outline sketch identifying
the highest peaks. By the time I revisited on 26 February 2011, this had been
replaced by a laminated sign titled 'Welcome to Auchessan' with a photograph
of the view north on which several hills are named. It will be found on a wooden
post on the south side of the River Dochart, a few yards from the bridge. The
photograph was taken from a few hundred metres south of where the sign has
been mounted, but all the features identified on it are visible.

## Dun More Hill                                      NN 766 234

Square printed panel on a cairn. Designed by Alan Dempster, erected by
Strathearn Ramblers and unveiled in the presence of ninety-five members and
friends on Sunday, 6 August 2000. Stones for the cairn were gathered from the
River Ruchill and taken up the hill by tractor, but for the last few yards had
to be carried by hand. During this operation Vice-Chair Margaret Shankland
slipped and fractured her ankle, which left her incapacitated for more than six
weeks. The cairn will be found a few yards from Lord Melville's monument, a
nineteenth century granite obelisk. The peak identified as Ormiston Hill 236m

must be something else. Ormiston Hill appears to the south of Mount Hill 221m, not to the north as the panel suggests.

'Millennium Cairn to be unveiled', *Strathearn Herald*, 4 August 2000

'Millennium Cairn in Comrie', *Strathearn Herald*, 11 August 2000

Scottish Natural Heritage, *Facts and Figures*, 2000/01, p.167

*Strathearn Rambler*, Summer Edition 2010, Issue No. 51

## Knock of Crieff   NN 867 229

Chromium plated copper disc, covered with glass, on an octagonal granite pillar. Designed by Duncan K. Paterson of Paisley and erected by Crieff Town Council in July 1930. The view indicator was a gift from an anonymous donor in memory of Robert Rule (1837–1929), a Glaswegian cloth manufacturer who had retired to Crieff. Tom S. Hall wrote that in preparing the indicator, 'photographs were taken on eight sides, hence the octagonal shape of the chart.'

The original disc has been replaced by a laminated one. Access to the pillar is by climbing the three steps of a stone platform. Beinn Each 813m and Uamh Bheag 664m are misidentified. Neither is visible.

'View Finder at Crieff', *The Scotsman*, 11 July 1930

'View Indicator for Crieff', *Strathearn Herald*, 12 July 1930

Tom S. Hall, 'How Mountain Indicator is Made', *The Courier and Advertiser*, 26 September 1930

'View Indicator at the Knock of Crieff', *Scottish Country Life*, Volume 17, October 1930, p. 326 (photo)

*Two young women examine the view indicator on the Knock of Crieff. Source: Scottish Country Life, 1930.*

# Corsiehill 

NO 136 235

Paper chart in a glass frame, with a protecting grid, mounted on a cast iron stand. Drawn by the solicitor John Ritchie and installed on Tuesday, 7 July 1903. Its condition was described as 'ruinous' in 1924. The chart was removed temporarily in the 1940s 'owing to the exigencies of war'. In 1947 a new indicator was installed at the site, a bronze plate on a stone plinth. The design of the bronze plate is a near copy of the paper original.

> 'The Horizon from Corsiehill', *Transactions and Proceedings of the Perthshire Society of Natural Science*, Volume 3, Part V, 1903, pp.245–248 (includes copy of paper chart)
>
> 'Here and There', *Evening Telegraph*, 21 August 1903
>
> 'Kinnoull Hill Revisited', *Perthshire Advertiser*, 2 August 1924, p.11
>
> 'Kinnoull Hill Charts', *Perthshire Advertiser*, 25 June 1947, p.8

*A bronze plate at Corsiehill, Perth describes the view north-west. Photo taken 24/08/2009.*

# Kinnoull Hill 

NO 136 228

Bronze disc on a stone cylinder. Designed by Perth burgh surveyor John Penman and erected by John L. Anderson c.1950. The indicator commemorates Lord Dewar's gift of the hill to the city.

The surveying work for the disc was carried out by the civil engineer Ben Oliphant, at the time an apprentice in Penman's office. Oliphant made several visits to the summit of Kinnoull with a theodolite and a heavy pair of binoculars that were obtained by the council from a captured German warship in the Second World War. After the disc was installed, a member of the public pointed out that the direction given for Kinnoull Hill Tower was about 30 degrees off. In response, Oliphant and Penman amended the label to 'Kinnoull Hill Tower Path'. The solution was ingenious but slippery: both Oliphant and Penman were aware that the path indicated did not lead to the tower.

Morton and Mair state that there was an indicator on the summit of Kinnoull before the Second World War. But there is curious absence of references to it in other sources, and Oliphant tells me there was no structure at the summit before the current bronze indicator erected c.1950. The most likely explanation for the statements in Morton and Mair seems to be confusion with the indicator at Corsiehill.

*The Courier* for 4 January 2011 reported that the Kinnoull Hill indicator had been struck by lightning; it has since been repaired. More than eighty features are shown on the disc; five are misidentified.

H.V. Morton, *In Search of Scotland*, 1929

William Mair 'Scottish View Indicators and Panoramas', *Scottish Geographical Magazine*, Volume 55, issue 2, March 1939, pp.102–107

'Kinnoull Hill Charts', *Perthshire Advertiser*, 25 June 1947, p.8

'Mountain Indicators: New Features on Kinnoull Hill, Perth', *The Scotsman*, 4 May 1950

*The Courier*, 4 January 2011 (picture of lightning damaged indicator)

'Indicator not 90 years old', Ben Oliphant, letter in *The Courier* for 8 January 2011

Personal communication, Ben Oliphant of Perth

Personal communication, Fergus Cook, Perth & Kinross Council, 7 March 2013

# Duke's Pass

NN 523 045

Laminated disc on a dressed stone plinth, which is attached to a semi-circular wall. The Duke's Pass indicator was designed by the architects James Shearer and Annand of Dumfermline. It was gifted to the Forestry Commission by the Carnegie Trust at the same time as David Marshall Lodge. The indicator and Lodge were formally handed over to the Commission on Tuesday, 16 August 1960.

Carnegie Trust, Annual Report for 1960, p.38

Record for 'Aberfoyle, David Marshall Lodge and Indicator', Canmore ID 131263 (Item SA 1950/36/26 includes drawings of view from where the indicator stands and the design of the face of the indicator)

# Loch Drunkie                                    NN 547 043

Metal plate on a wooden stand. Erected by the Forestry Commission. The Commission was unable to provide any information as to its date. The peak identified as Beinn a'Chroin 946m is Beinn a'Choin 770m. Beinn a'Chroin 946m is not visible.

> Personal communications, Stuart Chalmers and David Anderson, Forestry
>     Commission, 24 March 2010

# David Marshall Lodge                             NN 520 014

Steel plate on a stone plinth. Erected by the Automobile Association and unveiled on Monday, 13 May 1974. It stands a few yards south of David Marshall Lodge. There is also a telescope. Ben Venue is not visible.

> *Courier & Advertiser*, 14 May 1974 (photo of unveiling)

# Dunblane New Golf Club                           NN 788 002

Plastic panel on a wooden post. Erected by Dunblane New Golf Club in 1988 to mark the achievement of the late Mrs Kathleen Smith in winning the Ladies Championship on twenty occasions. Kathleen Smith first won the club championship in 1937 and was a formidable force in ladies golf at Dunblane for the next 35 years. The indicator is near the fifth tee of the course.

> Pat MacLachlan, *100 Years of Golf in Dunblane*, p.55
> Personal communication, Jim Montgomery, Match Secretary, Dunblane New
>     Golf Club

# Thornhill                                        NS 666 996

Panel on a stone plinth. Designed by students at Stirling University and erected by Scottish Natural Heritage c.1997 or 1998.

> Personal communication, David Pickett, SNH, 5 January 2011

*Loch Drunkie viewpoint. This metal plate, tucked away in forestry in the Trossachs, must be one of the least visited view indicators in Scotland. Photo taken 09/03/2010.*

*The Automobile Association's view indicator at David Marshall Lodge. The AA's indicators have quite a consistent style: a metal plate on a stone plinth. Lines engraved on the plate show the direction of surrounding features. Photo taken 11/04/2010.*

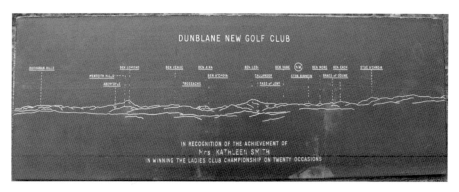

*A panel mounted at Dunblane New Golf Club identifies the hills to the west. Photo taken 16/12/2010.*

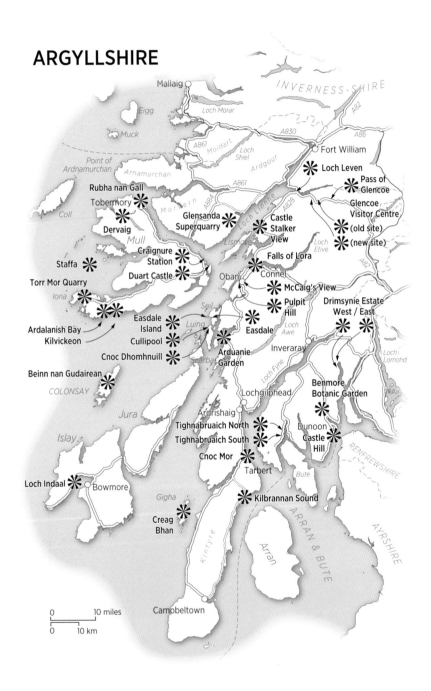

# ARGYLLSHIRE

INVERNESS-SHIRE

Mallaig

Loch Morar

*Eigg*

*Muck*

A830

Fort William

Point of Ardnamurchan

*Arnamurchan*

Loch Shiel

Moidart

Ardgour

A861

Loch Leven

Pass of Glencoe

Rubha nan Gall

Tobermory

Dervaig

*Coll*

*Mull*

Glensanda Superquarry

Castle Stalker View

Glencoe Visitor Centre
(old site)
(new site)

Loch Etive

A828

A82

Staffa

Torr Mor Quarry

*Iona*

Craignure Station

Duart Castle

Falls of Lora

Oban

Connel

McCaig's View

Pulpit Hill

Drimsynie Estate West / East

Loch Awe

Loch Lomond

Ardalanish Bay
Kilvickeon

Easdale Island

Cullipool

Cnoc Dhomhnuill

*Seil*

*Luing*

*Scarba*

Easdale

Arduanie Garden

Inveraray

Loch Fyne

Beinn nan Gudairean

*COLONSAY*

*Jura*

Benmore Botanic Garden

Lochgilphead

Ardrishaig

Tighnabruaich North

Tighnabruaich South

Cnoc Mor

Dunoon Castle Hill

RENFREWSHIRE

*Islay*

Tarbert

*Bute*

ARRAN & BUTE

AYRSHIRE

Loch Indaal

Bowmore

*Gigha*

Kilbrannan Sound

Creag Bhan

*Kintyre*

*Arran*

Campbeltown

0        10 miles

0      10 km

# Argyll

## Benmore Botanic Garden

NS 136 856

Metal plate mounted on two metal legs. Drawn by the architect David Mason ARIAS, and installed by the Royal Botanic Garden in the early 1990s. The peak identified as Dunrod Hill 298m is Creuch Hill 441m; the peak identified as Uig Hill 355m is also incorrect. The chimney of Inverkip Power Station, which is shown on the panel, was demolished at 10p.m. on Sunday, 28 July 2013.

> Personal communication, Jane McCrorie, Royal Botanic Garden, 21 October 2013

## Tighnabruaich North

NS 000 775

Metal plate on a boulder. This is one of a pair of indicators which were presented to the National Trust for Scotland by the Scottish Civic Trust in the summer of 1969, when the A8003 opened to the public. According to an inscription on the plates, they were erected 'in memory of two brothers who knew and loved Scotland and its mountains'. The brothers were Harry and Jack MacRobert, prominent members of the Scottish Mountaineering Club in the twenties and thirties. Harry edited several of the Club's guide books and was at one time President, while Jack edited the Club's journal for several years. The Tighnabruaich indicators were installed on the initiative of Michael MacRobert, who was Jack MacRobert's son and also a prime mover in setting up the Scottish Civic Trust.

> Obituary of Jack MacRobert, *Scottish Mountaineering Club Journal*, Vol. 24, No. 139, May 1948, p.66
>
> Obituary of Harry MacRobert, *Scottish Mountaineering Club Journal*, Vol. 25, No. 146, May 1955, pp.364–366
>
> *The Scots Magazine*, Volume 91, August 1969, p.458
>
> Obituary of Michael MacRobert, *Herald Scotland*, 28 March 2000
>
> Personal communication, David MacRobert of MacRoberts Solicitors in Glasgow
>
> Personal communications, Ian Riches, NTS, 4 and 9 June 2009

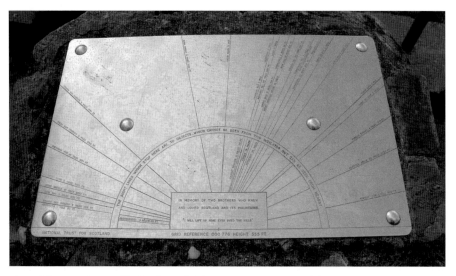

*One of the two plates at Tighnabruaich. This is the northern one. Photo taken 15/05/2009.*

## Castle Hill 

NS 175 763

Plastic disc on a stone cylinder. Extensive enquiries yielded no information about when the indicator on Castle Hill at Dunoon was installed or by whom. It was in place by March 1963, when it was noticed by an RCAHMS surveyor describing the remains of Dunoon Castle. The peak identified as Beinn Lagan is Cruach Bhuidhe; the peak identified as Ben Arthur (The Cobbler) is Beinn Narnain.

Record for 'Dunoon Castle' on RCAHMS database (Canmore ID 40729)

## Tighnabruaich South 

NR 992 746

Metal plate on a boulder. See Tighnabruaich North. Do not be deterred by the roadside sign stating that the path to this viewpoint is 'only for the fit and agile'. It is one of the easiest indicators in Scotland to reach.

## Cnoc Mor

NR 874 695

Metal disc mounted at ground level on a boulder. Erected by the Argyll & Bute Countryside Trust for Douglas & Valerie Barker of Barfad in the 1990s. The peak identified as Beinn Mhor 741m is Cruach nan Caorach 458m. Beinn Mhor is not visible. Access is by means of a rather steep and rough path which climbs from woods to the west.

## Loch Leven                                          NN 097 587

Framed paper chart on a stone plinth. Designed by Drew McClelland and erected
by Highland Council in January 2006. Three peaks are misidentified.

> Personal communication, Drew McClelland, Highland Council

## Glencoe Visitor Centre (new site)                    NN 112 575

Relief model on a viewing platform, erected by the National Trust for Scotland in
May 2002. Access to the viewing platform is through a visitor centre; there is no
charge but it is only accessible when the centre is open. There is also a telescope.

*A relief model at the National Trust for Scotland's new visitor centre
identifies the hills around Glencoe. Photo taken 02/04/2010.*

## Pass of Glencoe                                       NN 170 568

Triangular bronze plate on a stone plinth. This device was one of a pair installed
by the National Trust for Scotland in 2002 by way of advertising the new visitor
centre. They were located about 250 metres apart at lay-bys on the south side of

the A82 (grid references NN 170 568 and NN 168 569). In March 2013, the NTS replaced the triangular bronze plates with circular laminated panels, about 45 inches in diameter.

Personal communications, Scott McCombie, NTS, 1 June 2009 and Jo Anthony, NTS, 12 November 2013

## Rubha nan Gall       NM 508 568

Square bronze plate on a stone cube. Erected as a memorial to Robert John Brown (1873–1936), a Harris tweed merchant who lived in the house called Stronsaule in Tobermory. There is also a stone bench. Creag Bhan Ard 1101 feet and Beinn Dubh 424 feet are misidentified. Neither is visible.

'Death of Harris Tweed Merchant, Mr Robert John Brown of Tobermory', *The Scotsman*, 20 January 1936

Personal communication, Olive Brown, Stronsaule (Olive Brown is the wife of Robert Brown's late grandson), 13 January 2010

*The view from Rubha nan Gall on Mull has changed little since the 1930s. Photo taken 15/06/2009.*

## Glencoe Visitor Centre (old site)    NN 126 564

The National Trust for Scotland opened a visitor centre at Glencoe at this site in 1976. Steps led up to a viewing platform on the roof, which carried a panel with a labelled drawing of the view east to the mountains on either side of Glencoe. The visitor centre was removed when the new one was established in 2002, and there is no obvious physical evidence of it today. A slide dated 1977 in the NTS archive shows two children examining the panel.

Personal communication, John Sinclair, NTS, 2 March 2010

## Kilbrannan Sound    NR 862 552

Metal plate on a wooden post. Erected by the Argyll & Bute Countryside Trust c.1995.

Personal communication, Bill Middlemiss, Argyll & Bute Countryside Trust, 22 April 2009 (the Trust ceased operations in the late 1990s)

*Kilbrannan Sound Viewpoint, on the coast of Kintyre, looks across to Arran. Photo taken 14/05/2009.*

## Dervaig    NM 439 518

Metal plate on a wooden frame. Erected by the Argyll & Bute Countryside Trust in 1992/93. The island identified as Tiree is part of Coll. Tiree is not visible.

Personal communication, Bill Middlemiss, Argyll & Bute Countryside Trust, 4 July 2009

# Creag Bhan NR 647 509

Metal disc on a stone cairn. Erected by Argyll & Bute Council in March 2005. Ben More on Mull and Ben Cruachan are not visible.

'Spring Outdoor Access Week', News Release on Argyll & Bute Council website, 16 March 2005

*Disc at the summit of Creag Bhan on the Isle of Gigha. Despite its modest height (100m), the peak offers spectacular views of the west coast and Inner Hebrides. Photo taken 14/05/2009.*

# Glensanda Superquarry NM 813 502

Metal plate on a stone plinth. Designed by Iain Thornber, estate factor for Foster Yeoman Ltd, the company which is excavating Glensanda Superquarry. The device was funded by the company and installed in late 2003. The peak on Mull identified as Ben Buie is Creach Beinn. Ben Buie is not visible.

Personal communication, Iain Thornber, 23 March 2010 and 8 January 2011

# Castle Stalker View NM 925 477

Framed paper chart, about four feet long and two feet deep, on wooden legs.

Erected by Castle Stalker Café in 2005. It will be found a few yards to the south of the café.

Personal communication, Peter Blood, Osprey Signs, 7 January 2013

## Craignure Station

NM 723 369

Metal plate on a stone plinth. Erected by the Argyll & Bute Countryside Trust in 1994/95.

Personal communication, Bill Middlemiss, Argyll & Bute Countryside Trust, 4 July 2009

*A metal plate at Craignure Station on Mull identifies the hills of the mainland to the north-east. Photo taken 14/06/2009.*

## Duart Castle

NM 748 353

Two plastic panels, each on a wooden frame, mounted on the battlements of Duart Castle. One panel looks south west, the other east 'to the "Munros" and the big tops of Lochaber and Argyll'. They were commissioned by Sir Lachlan Maclean, designed by Jim Thomson Graphic Design of Muir of Ord and installed in the early 1990s. Access is by means of several flights of stairs inside the castle, which currently opens between April and October. There is a charge for admission. Fifteen of the twenty-eight land features named on the panels are misidentified.

Personal communication, Sir Lachlan Maclean, 15 May 2010 and John Young, 2bcreative, 9 December 2010

# Staffa                                        NM 325 351

Metal plate on a cairn made from recycled roofing slates, intended to evoke the hexagonal columns of Fingal's cave. Installed by the National Trust for Scotland and unveiled in the presence of a party of about eight (including a bagpiper) on Monday, 30 July 2012. Gribun, Bunessan and Fionnphort are hamlets on Mull. The croft of Burg, also on Mull, is not visible.

'New Cairn for Staffa', NTS Press Release, 26 July 2012

# Falls of Lora                               NM 909 343

Panel on a metal post. Erected by the Argyll & Bute Countryside Trust in 1993/94. A photo posted on Geograph suggests the panel survived until at least June 2005. When I visited on 17 May 2009 it was missing; the metal post remained. It will be found among gravel a few yards from the sea.

Personal communication, Bill Middlemiss, Argyll & Bute Countryside Trust, 4 July 2009

'Connel', photo taken in June 2005 by Mick Garratt on Geograph

# McCaig's View                             NM 860 302

Paper chart encased in clear plastic. Erected by the Group for Recycling in Argyll and Bute (GRAB) around 2003. The chart is mounted on the railings of a terrace on the west side of McCaig's Tower, a striking folly built on a hillside in Oban. When I visited on 2 April 2010, the chart was faded and difficult to read.

Minutes of Meeting of the Oban Common Good Fund, 15 November 2002

# Pulpit Hill                                 NM 853 295

Doulton stoneware disc on a block of dressed stone. Designed by the Burgh Surveyor David Galloway and erected by Oban Town Council in 1930. The summit of Pulpit Hill was closed to the public for the duration of the Second World War.

The disc shows a confusing mixture of visible and hidden features, with no guidance as to which is which. Describing the view from Pulpit Hill in an article published in 1933, Hugh Shedden wrote that: 'Uninterruptedly the eye can travel round fully half of the compass from south-west to north-east – a useful indicating dial on the hill crest, will give direction – with all the features within a radial distance of twenty-five miles being clearly visible in an ordinary atmosphere…'. Shedden specifically notes that Iona and Staffa, more than 25 miles distant, are not visible.

However, even within a 25 mile radius a number of features are not visible, in particular Creach Bheinn 810m, Meall Riaghain 626m and Cruach Airdeny 396m.

B.H. Humble, *Wayfaring Around Scotland*, p.199

'Oban – Its Story. Part XV', *The Oban Times*, Saturday, 28 October 1933 (reproduced as chapter XII of Hugh Shedden, *The Story of Lorn, Its Isles and Oban*, 1938)

'Oban Hill Open to Public', *Glasgow Herald*, 18 July 1945

## Topp Mop Quarry                                    NM 304 239

Panel on a stone plinth. Designed by the Mull-based company Unfolding Island Images and erected by the Ross of Mull Historical Centre in 2005.

Websites of Ross of Mull Historical Centre and Unfolding Island Images

*The view from Torr Mor quarry, half a mile north of Fionnphort on Mull. Photo taken 03/04/2010.*

## Kilvickeon                               NM 413 194

Panel on a stone plinth. Designed by Unfolding Island Images and erected by the Ross of Mull Historical Centre in 2005. The panel shows the view from higher ground in the vicinity of the nearby house of Scoor. From its current location, Malcolm's Point, the Garvellachs and Scarba are not visible.

## Ardalanish Bay                           NM 374 190

Panel on a metal post. Erected by the Argyll & Bute Countryside Trust, c.1994. The artist appears to have drawn the view from a higher position than where the panel now stands, but everything on the panel is visible from its current location.

> Personal communication, Bill Middlemiss, Argyll & Bute Countryside Trust, 4 July 2009

## Easdale Island                           NM 736 171

Bronze disc on a stone cylinder. Local residents believe the Easdale Island indicator was installed by the one-time owner of the island, Chris Nicholson, in the late 1970s or early 1980s. The intention was to distinguish visible and non-visible features by means of long and short arrows. Two features claimed by the disc to be visible are hidden by closer ground: Ben More on Mull and the Shepherd's Hat.

> Personal communication, Jim Watson, Slate Islands Heritage Trust, 23 April 2009

## Easdale                                  NM 755 169

Bronze disc on a stepped stone plinth. Erected by the people of Kilbrandon to commemorate the coronation of Queen Elizabeth II, June 1953.

## Cnoc Dhomhnuill                          NM 743 131

Metal disc mounted on top of an Ordnance Survey triangulation pillar. Designed by Peter Hooper and erected by the Isle of Luing Community Trust in 2008.

> Personal communication, Peter Hooper, Isle of Luing Community Trust

*The high point of Easdale Island. Photo taken 13/03/2010.*

# Cullipool
NM 738 130

Laminated panel on a stone plinth. Erected by the Isle of Luing Community Trust in 2008. The panel is titled 'Birds of Shore and Sea' and is sited at the 90 degree bend in the road through Cullipool. The island identified as Jura is Islay.

Personal communication, Peter Hooper, Isle of Luing Community Trust

# Arduanie Gardens
NM 792 102

Panel mounted on a metal frame. Erected by the National Trust for Scotland in 1997. It is marked as the 'New Viewpoint' on the map available at the entrance to Arduanie Gardens. The gardens are open daily throughout the year. There is a charge for admission.

# Drimsynie Estate East
NN 190 011

Framed paper chart on metal legs. Erected by Drimsynie Estate in 2008.

Personal communication, Laura Hardy, Drimsynie Estate, 1 May 2009

# Drimsynie Estate West
NN 186 006

Framed paper chart on metal legs. Erected by Drimsynie Estate in 2008.

# Beinn nan Gudairean
NR 388 949

Bronze disc on a stone cairn. The disc carried the inscription '445 feet above sea level. Erected 1938. Scale 1 inch = 6 miles. Drawn by James Macaulay MTPI, FSI, FSA'. Enquiries yielded no definite information as to who installed this device. It appears to have been put up with little publicity – it was not noticed, for example, by Humble or Mair. The disc showed the direction and distance of twelve landscape features including 'Irish Free State, 65 miles'. Topographically, this is accurate, as some of the Donegal hills are visible. Politically, it was out of date even when the indicator was installed: the Irish Free State had ceased to exist the year before.

The disc was present on 21 August 2008, when I visited, but it was reported stolen on 9 June 2012 and has not since been replaced.

'More metal theft: Colonsay loses valuable historic bronze plate', *ForArgyll* (online newspaper), 9 June 2012

# Loch Indaal

NR 264 610

Metal plate on a stone plinth. Designed by Dr. Julie Watson and erected by the Argyll & Bute Countryside Trust in the 1990s. By February 2011, some of the stones in the plinth had come loose, but the plate was still in place.

*Loch Indaal Viewpoint on the Isle of Islay. On a clear day, there are views of the Paps of Jura. Photo taken 25/02/2011.*

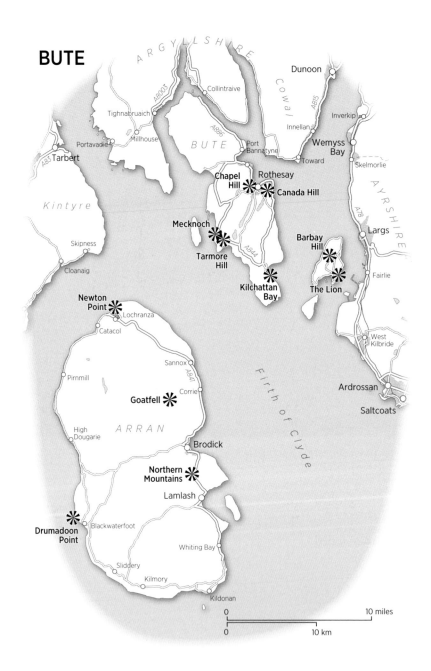

# BUTE

ARGYLLSHIRE

Dunoon

Collintraive

Tighnabruaich

COWAL

Inverkip

Portavadie

Millhouse

BUTE

Port
Bannatyne

Wemyss
Bay

Tarbert

Innellan

Toward

Skelmorlie

Kintyre

Chapel
Hill

Rothesay

Canada Hill

AYRSHIRE

Skipness

Mecknoch

Barbay
Hill

Largs

Cloanaig

Tarmore
Hill

Kilchattan
Bay

The Lion

Fairlie

Newton
Point

Lochranza

West
Kilbride

Catacol

Sannox

Pirnmill

Corrie

Firth of Clyde

Ardrossan

Goatfell

ARRAN

Saltcoats

High
Dougarie

Brodick

Northern
Mountains

Drumadoon
Point

Blackwaterfoot

Lamlash

Sliddery

Whiting Bay

Kilmory

Kildonan

0                    10 miles

0                    10 km

# Bute

## Chapel Hill ⚲

NS 083 648

Bronze plate on a stone plinth. The plate carries the inscription D.N.M DEL 1937.

The *Rothesay Express* reported that the indicator was gifted to Rothesay Town Council by a Dr Marshall. This is believed to be Dr. John Nairn Marshall of Rothesay, and the proposed identification for D.N.M., the plate's designer, is his daughter Dorothy Nairn Marshall (1900–1992). Four features are misidentified.

'Indicator at Chapelhill', *Rothesay Express*, 12 October 1937

Personal communication, Glyn Collis, Bute Museum, 23 November 2009

*A sign in Rothesay shows the way to the Chapel Hill. Photo taken 16/05/2009.*

## Canada Hill ⚲

NS 100 643

Metal plate in a concrete frame, set on a concrete tube. Erected by Argyll & Bute District Council c.1984. The plate is in the same style as Mecknoch. The Crosbie Hills are misidentified.

Countryside Commission for Scotland, *Seventeenth Report*, 1984, p. 32

## Mecknoch ⚲

NS 044 593

Metal plate on a wooden board, set on a metal stand. Erected by Argyll & Bute District Council c.1984. By May 2009, the wooden board was detached from the stand. The feature identified as Mainland Kintrye is Knapdale.

Countryside Commission for Scotland, *Seventeenth Report*, 1984, p. 32

# Tarmore Hill  NS 050 588

Metal plate on a stone cube. Produced by Argyll & Bute Countryside Trust for Argyll & Bute Council and SNH. Archie Crawford tells me it was erected during the early part of 1997. Three peaks are misidentified.

> Personal communication, Archie Crawford, Argyll & Bute Council, 5 June 2009

# Barbay Hill  NS 167 570

Bronze plate on a stone cube. Donated in 1953 by Samuel Irvine Paul (1891–1976) of 'Rock Villa' in Millport, a retired engineer who had worked in Alexander Stephen and Son shipyard in Glasgow. The Paps of Jura and Corsewall Point are not visible.

> J.R.D. Campbell, *Millport and the Cumbraes*, 2nd edition, 2004, p. 13
>
> Personal communication, Professor Geoff Moore, University Marine Biological Station Millport, 8 January 2010

# Kilchattan Bay  NS 103 549

Polished granite half disc on a stone cairn. Designed by William and Tom McKirdy and erected by the Kingarth and Kilchattan Bay Improvements Committee in 2000 to mark the Millennium. *The Buteman* reported that the cairn 'will be topped with directional pointer detailing the views across the Clyde'. None of the features named are visible; the distance and direction given for Ailsa Craig are hopelessly wrong; the distance given for Largs would have the effect of re-locating the town to Great Cumbrae Island. In fairness to those responsible, no tax-payer money was involved.

> 'A Sign of the Times', *The Buteman*, 14 January 2000
>
> Personal communication, Mrs Norrie Towers, Kingarth and Kilchattan Bay Improvements Committee, 29 December 2010

# The Lion  NS 179 549

Metal plate on a concrete plinth. Erected by North Ayrshire Council in 1998. Rigging Hill and Glentane Hill are misidentified. The farmhouse of Howcraig is not visible.

> Personal communication, Richard Henry, North Ayrshire Council, 19 June 2009

*Above: Viewpoint at Grantown-on-Spey. The indicator was originally installed in 1914. Photo taken 19/05/2009.*

*Right: The so-called Tillicoultry Hill indicator, erected in 1929. Since this photo was taken (1962), the device has been removed. Source: James Allan*

Left: Valentine postcard shows the indicator at Pulpit Hill, Oban, installed in 1930

Middle left: Postcard published by Burn & Cox, Killiecrankie shows the Queen's View, Loch Tummel. This indicator was installed by the Automobile Association in 1957.

Bottom left: J. Arthur Dixon postcard titled 'Mountain Indicator and Chairlift, Glenshee, Perthshire'.

Top right: The tower on Corstorphine Hill, Edinburgh. Two bronze plates were installed on the pigeon turret in December 1933. Photo taken 12/05/2010.

Right: The indicator on Auchenlone (or East Mount Lowther), unveiled in May 1944. Photo taken 02/02/2010.

*Above left: The Kinnoull Hill indicator near Perth was erected c.1950. The Dundee Courier for 4 January 2011 reported that it had been struck by lightning. The plinth has since been repaired. Source: Dundee Courier*

*Above right: The Easdale indicator (1953), with its distinctive stepped plinth. Photo taken 13/3/2010.*

*Below: On a fine day, the view from Nairn beach extends as far North as Caithness. Photo taken 20/05/2009.*

*Opposite page: Allermuir Hill, a superb viewpoint within easy reach of Edinburgh. Photo taken 4/12/2009.*

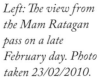

*Left: The view from the Mam Ratagan pass on a late February day. Photo taken 23/02/2010.*

*Middle left: The old Glencoe Visitor Centre was opened in 1976. Since this photo was taken (1977), the Centre has been demolished. Source: National Trust for Scotland.*

*Bottom left: Looking towards Skye from the Loch Alsh viewpoint. Photo taken 23/02/2010.*

*Top right: The indicator on Foula, Shetland is heavily defended by Bonxies. Photo taken 24/06/2010.*

*Bottom right: The indicator on Beinn Scrien, Eriskay takes the form of a disc attached to the top of an Ordnance Survey triangulation pillar. Photo taken 18/04/2010.*

*Above: Lady Hill, Elgin. Photo taken 01/02/2011.*

*Below: Inaugurating the indicator on Staffa, 30 July 2012. Source: National Trust for Scotland.*

# Newton Point

NR 931 515

Plastic disc on a stone cylinder. Erected by the Arran Coastal Way Support Group, c.2004/05.

> Community Outdoor Access Grants Scheme, table of grants awarded in 2004/05, on North Ayrshire Council website

# Goatfell

NR 991 415

Paper chart in glass frame, set on a stone cube. Designed by Duncan K. Paterson (assisted by Tom S. Hall) and erected by the Brodick Improvement Trust. The indicator was a gift from the *Daily Record*. Between 250 and 300 people attended the unveiling ceremony of Saturday, 10 August 1929, a day of driving mist and rain. At the conclusion of the ceremony they linked hands and sang 'Auld Lang Syne'. When Humble visited in May 1938 the indicator was derelict, with all that remained the metal frame round which the plinth had been built. The indicator has since been repaired by the Rotary Club of Kilwinning. Paterson's original design was inscribed on a metal plate and attached to a rebuilt plinth.

> 'Duke of Montrose at Goatfell Indicator Ceremony', *Daily Record*, 12 August 1929
>
> Tom S. Hall, *Tramping Holidays in Scotland*, 1933 pp.5–7
>
> B.H. Humble, 'A Day on the Arran Peaks', *Evening Times*, 7 May 1938
>
> Tom S. Hall, *Tramping in Arran*, 3rd edition, 1947, pp.34–38 (includes reproduction of the chart)

# Northern Mountains

NS 018 336

Metal plate on a stone plinth. Erected by North Ayrshire Council in 1996/97.

> Personal communication, Richard Henry, North Ayrshire Council, 19 June 2009

# Drumadoon Point

NR 882 288

Metal disc with labelled drawing on boulder by the shore. Erected as a family memorial in 1988. The Bastard, a 188m hill on the Mull of Kintyre, is indeed visible. But Paterson's Rock, a tidal island about a mile east of Sanda, is not.

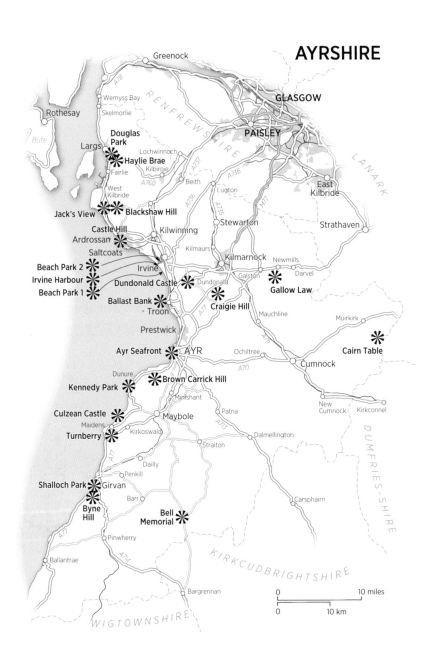

AYRSHIRE

Greenock

GLASGOW

Rothesay

Bute

Wemyss Bay

Skelmorlie

PAISLEY

RENFREWSHIRE

LANARK

Largs

Douglas
Park

Haylie Brae

Lochwinnoch

Kilbirnie

Fairlie

West
Kilbride

Beith

Lugton

East
Kilbride

Jack's View

Blackshaw Hill

Kilwinning

Stewarton

Strathaven

Castle Hill

Ardrossan

Saltcoats

Kilmaurs

Kilmarnock

Newmills

Beach Park 2

Irvine Harbour

Beach Park 1

Irvine

Dundonald Castle

Dundonald

Galston

Darvel

Gallow Law

Ballast Bank

Troon

Craigie Hill

Mauchline

Muirkirk

Prestwick

Ayr Seafront

AYR

Ochiltree

A70

Cumnock

Cairn Table

Kennedy Park

Dunure

Brown Carrick Hill

Minishant

Patna

New
Cumnock

Kirkconnel

Culzean Castle

Maidens

Maybole

Kirkoswald

Turnberry

Straiton

Dalmellington

DUMFRIES-SHIRE

Dailly

Penkill

Shalloch Park

Girvan

Barr

Carsphairn

Byne
Hill

Bell
Memorial

Pinwherry

Ballantrae

KIRKCUDBRIGHTSHIRE

Bargrennan

WIGTOWNSHIRE

0        10 miles

0        10 km

# Ayrshire

## Shalloch Park

NX 182 963

Panel on a stone cube. Erected by Girvan and South Carrick Social Inclusion Partnership in 2003. Bennane Head and Rathlin Island are not visible.

*Shalloch Park. The bun-like shape of Aisla Craig looms on the horizon. Photo taken 31/01/2010.*

## Byne Hill

NX 178 945

Bronze disc on a stone cairn. Erected by Girvan and District Round Table to commemorate the tercentenary of the Burgh of Girvan, 1668–1968. Islay, the Isle of Man and the Mull of Galloway are not visible. Ben Lomond is marginal.

# Bell Memorial

NX 352 906

Bronze relief model on a stone cube, set on a cobbled platform. A memorial to the cyclist David Bell (1907–1965) who became locally well-known through a column in the *Ayrshire Post* under the name 'The Highwayman'. Funded by public subscription and unveiled in May 1966. Since then, the view has become increasingly restricted by the coniferous forestry plantations which Bell detested.

'In Memory of a Highwayman', *Cycling*, 21 May 1966

David E.T. Bell, *The Highway Man*, 1970, p.16 (includes picture of unveiling ceremony)

*The Bell Memorial. Photo taken 31/01/2010.*

# Douglas Park

NS 214 585

Cardboard disc, framed in glass, on a concrete cylinder. Erected by Largs Town Council in July 1914. The original has been replaced with an engraved metal disc covered with a plastic shield. Several postcards from the 1970s carry pictures of this indicator. Ben Lomond 974m, Hill of Stake 522m, Misty Law 510m and Burnt Hill 486m are not visible.

'Observation Station for Douglas Park', *Largs & Millport Weekly*, 13 September 1913

Largs Burgh, Council Minutes, for 8 September 1913, 9 March and 11 May 1914

'Observation Station in Douglas Park', *Largs & Millport Weekly*, 14 March 1914

'Town Council Meetings – Works', *Largs & Millport Weekly*, 18 July 1914, p.3 (pedestal announced as erected)

# Haylie Brae ⚡

NS 215 582

Framed paper chart on a brick plinth. Designed and constructed by the Ardrossan-based training agency BEST, which was running an employment scheme with funding from Cunninghame District Council. The indicator was declared open twice in June 1989 following a dispute between BEST and the Council. After one of the Councillors accused BEST of 'training people for a profit', the Council decided not to invite BEST to the opening ceremony. BEST retaliated by organising a separate ceremony.

'Haylie Brae's different point of view', *Largs & Millport Weekly*, 30 June 1989

# Blackshaw Hill

NS 227 484

Metal plate on a stone cube. Erected by Bill Weir of Blackshaw Farm Park, c.1986. Blackshaw Farm Park operated as a visitor attraction, catering especially for children, between 1986 and 2000. Ben Lomond is not visible.

'Children's farm sold off to highest bidder', *Evening Times*, 27 October 2000

Personal communication, John Weir, Blackshaw Farm, 1 April 2010

*Summit of Blackshaw Hill. Photo taken 01/02/2010.*

# Jack's View

NS 200 482

Metal plate mounted on a boulder. The boulder stands on a paved viewing platform, which incorporates a bench sheltered by a stone wall. It is on the south side of Corsehill Drive. Erected by West Kilbride Civic Society, and unveiled on Saturday, 26 September 1987 in the presence of more than 150 people. The facility was built as a tribute to Dr Bill Jack, a biology teacher at Ardrossan Academy. On Saturday, 27 July 2013 the Civic Society unveiled a new plate. The feature identified as the Isle of Bute is part of Kintyre; the feature identified as Garroch Head (Bute) is on the Kintrye coast.

'West Kilbride pays tribute', *Largs & Millport Weekly*, 2 October 1987

West Kilbride Civic Society website

# Castle Hill                                    NS 231 423

Perspex covered chart on a stone plinth. Erected as part of a Manpower Services Commission programme with funding from Cunninghame District Council. Unveiled on Wednesday, 30 July 1986, it was vandalised within 10 days. It was still missing when I visited on 15 June 2010; the plinth remained.

'Viewfinder on hill', *Ardrossan & Saltcoats Herald*, 1 August 1986

'Viewfinder smashed', *Ardrossan & Saltcoats Herald*, 8 August 1986

*Derelict indicator at Castle Hill, Ardrossan. Photo taken 15/06/2010.*

# Beach Park F2                                  NS 305 380

Irvine Beach Park was created from a derelict industrial site from 1975 onwards. The work was done by Irvine Development Corporation and Cunninghame District Council. One of the elements of the redevelopment was the creation of two 'Panoramic View Signs' at sites called F1 and F2 in the plans. According to a contemporary schedule of works, these carried 'a panoramic view identifying the main features around the Beach Park'. Designed by the graphic artist Susan Stewart, the signs were erected in April 1982. Both were missing when I visited on 9 May 2009. At F2, there was no physical evidence either of the sign or the plinth on which it stood; at F1 there was a white metal cylinder which presumably was a plinth.

Irving Development Corporation, *Irvine Beach Park: Survey of existing and future signs*, 1:2500 scale map dated 6 August 1979

Irving Development Corporation, Irvine Beach Park, Minutes of Working Party Meetings for 29 September 1981 and 15 April 1982

## Irvine Harbour  NS 302 378

Metal disc on a concrete cylinder. Erected by the Irvine Development Corporation to mark the completion of the Harbour Wharf Restoration in 1992. It will be found on a viewing platform at the end of the breakwater. Pladda, a tiny island to the south of Arran, is just below the sea-horizon in conditions of normal refraction. (The lighthouse might perhaps be visible.)

## Beach Park F1 NS 308 374

See Beach Park F2.

## Gallow Law NS 531 353

Metal disc incorporated into a cairn. The cairn is an elaborate structure reached by four steps, with memorial tablets, viewing-mirrors and a weather vane. It was built by local coal miners during the General Strike as a memorial to the Covenanter James Smith (d. 1684). 'Well over 500 souls' were present at the unveiling ceremony, which took place on Saturday, 27 November 1926, praise being led by Galston Burgh Band and Massed Choir. The cairn has been renovated several times, most recently in May 2008 and is currently in good repair. Tinto, Cairn Table and Corsencon Hill are not visible.

*The cairn on Gallow Law. Source: Irvine Valley News, 19 November 1926.*

'The Cairn at Hillend', *Irvine Valley News*, 19 November 1926

'Covenanting Cairn', *Irvine Valley News*, 26 November 1926

'Unveiling of Covenanting Cairn at Gallow Hill', *Irvine Valley News*, 3 December 1926

## Dundonald Castle NS 364 345

Bronze disc on a concrete cylinder. Erected by the Friends of Dundonald Castle in association with Historic Scotland and South Ayrshire Council in April 1997. Aisla Craig and The Merrick are not visible.

Record for 'Dundonald Castle' on RCAHMS database (Canmore ID 41970)

Personal communication, Ken Gray, Friends of Dundonald Castle, 29 May 2009

*A disc mounted at Dundonald Castle gives directions for eighteen landscape features. Photo taken 09/05/2009.*

## Craigie Hill

NS 422 327

Bronze disc on a stone cylinder, which was reached by stone steps. Erected by the Kilmarnock Glenfield Ramblers Society and unveiled on Saturday, 5 June 1915 in the presence of about 1,500 people. The indicator was a memorial to Rev. Dr. David Landsborough (1826–1912), an amateur naturalist who was the Honorary President of the Society at the time of his death.

*The Landsborough Memorial on Craigie Hill. Source: Annals of the Kilmarnock Glenfield Ramblers Society, 1913–1919*

It showed the direction of 68 points of interest and also featured a likeness of Landsborough. The disc was stolen on 16 March 1966. Since then, the plinth and a large part of Craigie Hill (including the summit) have been destroyed in quarrying operations.

'Unveiling of the Landsborough Memorial', *Annals of the Kilmarnock Glenfield Ramblers Society*, 1913–1919, pp.10–19

Robert Currie, 'Landsborough Memorial on Craigie Hill', *Annals of the Kilmarnock Glenfield Ramblers Society*, 1913–1919, pp.20–29

David L. Richardson, *Kilmarnock Glenfield Ramblers Society: Centenary Annals 1884–1984*, 1983 pp.51–53

## Ballast Bank ⚑                                        NS 311 309

Steel disc on a stone cylinder. Erected by Troon Community Council in 1983. The cylinder is set on a stepped viewing platform. The orientation of the disc is not ideal (e.g. the engraved line to Ailsa Craig), but the indicator is still useful.

## Cairn Table                                        NS 724 242

Metal disc on a stone cylinder. Erected by Muirkirk Enterprise Group in 2005.

## Ayr Seafront                                        NS 330 215

Steel plate, about 4¼ feet long by 1 foot wide, attached to the sea wall on the esplanade at Ayr. Designed by Robert Lambert and his wife together with the Ocean Agency. Erected by Ayr, Fort, Seafield and Wallacestone Community Council in July 2009. The image on the plate corresponds (approximately) to what would be seen from a hypothetical mountain located a few miles east of Ayr. From the plate's actual position near sea level, several of the features depicted are not visible.

'Ayr Seafront Panoramic Plaque Unveiled', press release added to South Ayrshire Council website on 18 August 2009

Personal communication, Robert Lambert, Ayr, Fort, Seafield and Wallacestone Community Council, 17 April 2010

## Brown Carrick Hill ⚑                                        NS 299 164

Metal plate on a stone plinth. Both the installer and date are uncertain. It seems most likely that this device was erected by Kyle & Carrick District Council in the mid-1980s. Two strands of evidence support this theory. First, there is a reference to a grant being given to Kyle & Carrick District Council for a viewfinder in 1984. Second, there is a viewpoint symbol at this location on the 1987 edition of the Ordnance Survey map *Western & Central Scotland*, but not the 1984 edition. South Ayrshire Council (the successor to Kyle & Carrick District Council) was unable to provide any information.

When I visited on 9 May 2009, the plate was missing; the plinth remained. Jean McGinn told me that locals remember the plate being present about ten years ago.

Countryside Commission for Scotland, *Seventeenth Report*, 1984, p. 33

Personal communication, Jean McGinn, Dunure Community Council, 6 April 2010

## Kennedy Park                                                           NS 250 156

Metal plate on a stone plinth. Erected by Kyle & Carrick District Council in 1986 with funding from the Manpower Services Commission. The low-lying island of Inchmarnock is just below the sea horizon in conditions of normal refraction.

*Tucked away among gorse bushes, the indicator at Kennedy Park in Dunure. Photo taken 09/05/2009.*

# Culzean Castle                                    NS 233 103

A painted wooden board, perhaps six feet long, mounted on the clock tower of Culzean Castle. Erected by the National Trust for Scotland. The Trust is unsure as to its date but it is mentioned in Pennyfather's *Guide* of 1975. Because of the difficulty of accessing the clock tower, the board was moved to a new site on the battlements of the sea wall. It was still there when I visited the castle on 10 May 2009, but had become faded; it has since been removed. The board looked north-west to Arran and the Mull of Kintyre and was viewed from a platform with two ornamental cannons. At present, Culzean Castle is open daily from April to October. There is an admission charge.

> Keith Pennyfather, *Guide to Countryside Interpretation: Part two*, 1975, p.91
>
> Personal communication, Gordon Nelson, NTS

# Turnberry                                         NS 215 058

Metal disc on a stone cube. Designed by South Ayrshire Council and installed in 2004 as part of a Scottish Executive contract to build a climbing lane and new lay-by on the A77. Sanda Island and the Mull of Kintyre were not visible when I visited on 10 May 2009. Whether the sightlines were obstructed by land or the spring foliage of the adjacent hedgerow is not clear. (Results from digital models as to whether land blocks the view are so sensitive to the exact location and height from which the observation is made that they are probably not to be relied on.)

> 'A77 improvements at Turnberry', Scottish Executive press release, 19 March 2004

*A disc mounted at a lay-by on the A77 near Turnberry. Photo taken 10/05/2009.*

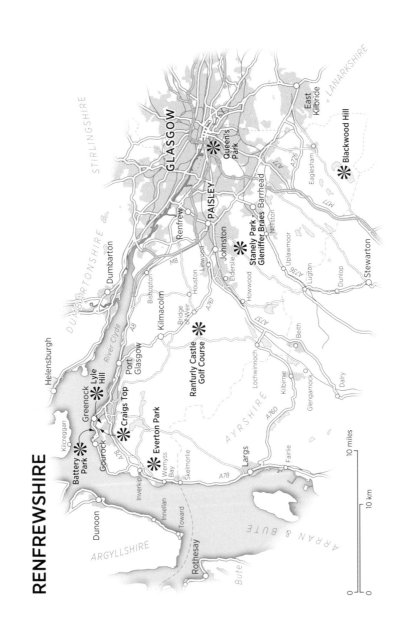

# RENFREWSHIRE

# RENFREWSHIRE

## Battery Park                                    NS 252 776

Metal oval on a stone plinth. Erected by Cardwell Bay & Greenock West Community Council in 2008. Four features are misidentified. Most notably, the hill identified as Ben Lomond is Beinn a'Mhanaich, one of the Luss Hills. Ben Lomond is not visible.

## Craigs Top                                      NS 256 771

Copper disc, chromium plated and covered with glass, on a stone cylinder. Designed by the town planner James Macaulay, MTPI, FSI and erected by the Greenock Ramblers Club with the assistance of the *Daily Record* and friends. Pipers played at the unveiling ceremony of Saturday, 24 April 1937. The indicator was sited 'near the flag pole at the Lyle Road'. This flag pole will be found on the east side of the

*Unveiling the view indicator on Craigs Top, Greenock. Source: The Greenock Telegraph, 26 April 1937*

road. When I visited on 1 February 2010, there were two suitable stone cylinders within about ten yards of the pole. Neither carried a disc.

Minutes of the Finance and General Purposes Committee, Greenock Corporation, 14 April 1936

'View Indicator on Lyle Hill', *The Greenock Telegraph*, 26 April 1937

'New View Indicator: Presentation Ceremony at Greenock', *The Glasgow Herald*, 26 April 1937

Greenock Ramblers Club, *Chart of View Indicator on Craigs' Top, Greenock* (available in the Watt Library, Greenock)

## Lyle Hill                                     NS 256 771

Metal disc mounted on a windlass. Erected
by the Automobile Association and unveiled
on Friday, 31 May 1985. It is sited near metal
railings on the west side of Lyle Road. Although they share a six figure grid reference,
the Craigs Top and Lyle Hill sites are about
75 metres apart, and separated by the Lyle
Road. Cnoc na h-Airighe 219m is not visible.

> 'On a clear day...', *The Greenock Telegraph*, 1
> June 1985

## Everton Park                    NS 218 710

Copper disc, chromium plated and covered
with glass, on a stone cylinder. Designed by
Duncan K. Paterson and presented by the
*Daily Record* to the Greenock District Boy
Scouts Association. Unveiled on Saturday, 19
May 1934. When I visited on 12 May 2009,

*The Automobile Association's
indicator at Lyle Hill, Greenock.
Photo taken 01/02/2010.*

the disc was missing but the plinth remained. Jim Bell told me that the disc
was vandalised some time after 2000, and is currently being held in storage by
the Greenock & District Scouts. It is engraved with the Scout Badge in the
centre and has a labelled outline of mountains around the edge. A report in the
*Greenock Telegraph* suggests that a film of the 1934 unveiling ceremony was made.
Regrettably this has not been traced.

> 'The Boy Scouts', *The Greenock Telegraph*, 15 May 1934
>
> 'Mountain View Indicator', *The Greenock Telegraph*, 21 May 1934
>
> 'Daily Record Gift to Boy Scouts', *Daily Record*, 21 May 1934
>
> Tom S. Hall, *Citizen Rambles: Byways and Uplands*, undated (the labelled
> drawing of the view from the Everton Park indicator by D.K. Paterson at
> pp.16–17 is not a reproduction of the disc)
>
> Personal communication, Jim Bell, Greenock & District Scouts, 26 October
> 2009 (I am grateful to Jim Bell for supplying me with photographs of the disc)

## Ranfurly Castle Golf Course                    NS 372 652

Paper chart in a glass frame on a stone plinth. Designed by Charles Hogg of

*Unveiling the indicator at Everton Park Scout Camp.*
*Source: The Greenock Telegraph, 21 May 1934*

Bridge of Weir and presented by Lewis Clapperton, Captain of Ranfurly Castle Golf Club. Erected on Tuesday, 1 November 1927. The paper chart was replaced by a metal plate of similar design c.1990. A copy of the paper original hangs in the stairwell of the clubhouse. When I visited on 9 May 2009, trees planted on the course impaired the 'fifty-mountain view' celebrated by Humble and Hall in the thirties. Ben Vane 915m would not be visible even if they were removed.

Tom S. Hall, 'Fifty Mountains: A Renfrewshire Vantage Point', in *Citizen Rambles: Byways and Uplands*

Personal communication, Clive Cummings, Ranfurly Castle Golf Club, 16 October 2009

# Queen's Park NS 579 620

Metal plate mounted on railings. Erected by Glasgow City Council in early 2006. It will be found a few yards from the flagstaff. A circular panorama from this site was published more than a hundred years before. On the current plate, the peak identified as Ben Lomond is Stob Binnein. It is doubtful whether Ben Lomond is visible, but if it is, you would need binoculars to see it.

Anon, *Panorama views from the Flagstaff, Queen's Park, Glasgow* (17¼ inches x 17¼ inches), c.1903

Personal communication, Ian Fraser, Glasgow City Council, 28 April 2010 and Kathy Archer, Hockerill Engraving, 8 December 2010

## Stanely Park, Gleniffer Braes   NS 457 606

Bronze plate on a pink granite plinth. Designed by James Donald and erected by John Robertson of Robertson & Sons preserve manufacturers in July 1911. Ten years after the indicator was installed, Duncan K. Paterson drew an outline of the hills as seen from the dial, which was sold as a printed panorama. The gift of the indicator by the Robertson family was roughly contemporary with the introduction of the 'Golly' mascot to market their jams and marmalades. In honour of the family's achievements, Stanely Park (in which the indicator stands) was renamed as Robertson Park. Eight of the features on the plate are not visible.

'The Treasurer's Gift', *Paisley and Renfrewshire Gazette*, 15 July 1911

D.K. Paterson and Herbert Priestley, *Outline of Hills as Seen from the Gleniffer Braes South of Paisley*, chart published by the Paisley Naturalists Society, June 1921

D.K. Paterson, *Chart of the Hills as seen from the Gleniffer Braes at Braehead*, Paisley Naturalists Society, 1935

Jerry Loader, *The Folly of Golly*, 2005 (superb illustrated work by a leading Golly historian – a photo of the Gleniffer Braes indicator is at p.24)

## Blackwood Hill   NS 543 483

Bronze disc on a stone cylinder. Designed by Stephen Pardue of Differentia Design, erected by East Renfrewshire Council and unveiled on Thurday, 26 July 2012. The disc was based on a digital panorama made by Jonathan de Ferranti of Newburgh.

'Join Whitelee to see the sea', *Glasgow South and Eastwood Extra, 31 July 2012*

*The indicator on Blackwood Hill is the most detailed in Scotland. The disc identifies 140 landscape features. Photo taken 27/12/2012.*

# DUMBARTONSHIRE

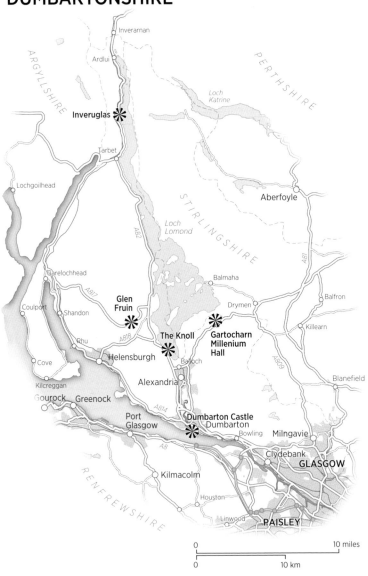

ARGYLLSHIRE

PERTHSHIRE

Inverarnan

Ardlui

Loch
Katrine

Inveruglas ✳

Tarbet

Lochgoilhead

Aberfoyle

STIRLINGSHIRE

Loch
Lomond

A82

Garelochhead

Balmaha

Balfron

Glen
Fruin ✳

Drymen

Coulport

Shandon

Killearn

The Knoll ✳

Gartocharn
Millenium
Hall ✳

A818

Rhu

Balloch

Helensburgh

A809

Cove

Alexandria

Blanefield

Kilcreggan

Gourock    Greenock

A814

Dumbarton Castle ✳

Port
Glasgow

Dumbarton

Bowling    Milngavie

A8

Clydebank

GLASGOW

RENFREWSHIRE

Kilmacolm

Houston

Linwood

PAISLEY

0 ——————————————— 10 miles

0 ——————————————— 10 km

# DUMBARTONSHIRE

## Inveruglas

NN 323 098

Bronze disc on a stone column. Erected by Dumbarton District Council c.1981. A memorial to Thomas Johnston (1881–1965), the Labour politician who created the North of Scotland Hydro-Electric Board. Ben Vane is not visible.

> Countryside Commission for Scotland, *Thirteenth Report*, 1980 p.32
> Countryside Commission for Scotland, *Fourteenth Report*, 1981 p.36

## Glen Fruin

NS 331 866

Metal disc on a stone cairn. Erected by Strathclyde Regional Council in 1995, when the A817 was opened to the public. By the time I visited, on 16 May 2009, the disc was missing; the cairn remained.

> Personal communication, Stephen Doogan, Argyll & Bute Council, 21 February 2011

## Gartocharn Millennium Hall

NS 428 863

Metal plate on a sandstone plinth. Erected by Kilmaronock Community Trust and inaugurated during a Christmas lunch that took place in the adjacent hall on Sunday, 16 December 2012. The plate carries an annotated photograph by Doug Akhurst, showing the view towards Loch Lomond. The device will be found on a terrace on the north side of the hall.

> 'Top o' the day...the new Toposcope is launched at the Millennium Hall', *Dumpling Times*, Volume 16 number 5, February/March 2013.

## The Knoll

NS 372 832

Panel on a stone wall. Erected by the Friends of Loch Lomond c.1986. When I visited on 16 May 2009, the panel was missing, but the stone wall of the viewing

*Derelict view indicator at the Knoll, Duck Bay. Photo taken 16/05/2009.*

platform remained, encrusted with moss and ivy, hidden among trees. The site is reached by steps from Duck Bay car park.

Countryside Commission for Scotland, *Nineteenth Report*, 1986 p.67

## Dumbarton Castle

NS 399 744

Bronze disc on a stone plinth. Designed by J. Wilson Paterson (of H.M. Office of Works), erected by the London-Dumbartonshire Association and unveiled on Thursday, 30 March 1933. B.H. Humble's favourite viewpoint. Four peaks are misidentified.

The bronze disc has been supplemented by two panels, which carry annotated views painted in 2008. They are titled:

1.  Looking North-West (NS 399 745), mounted next to the cannon at the Duke of York's Battery;

2.  Looking North (NS 400 745), mounted on metal railings near to the three cannons of the Duke of Argyll's Battery.

Dumbarton Castle is open all year, but there is an admission charge.

*Unveiling Ceremony of Direction Finder (Mountain Indicator) on Dumbarton Rock*, programme published by London-Dumbartonshire Association

'London Society's Gift to Dumbarton', *The Scotsman*, 18 March 1933

'Indicator on Dumbarton Castle', *The Lennox Herald*, 1 April 1933

*A visitor examines the 1933 indicator at Dumbarton Castle. Photo taken 13/06/2009.*

# STIRLINGSHIRE

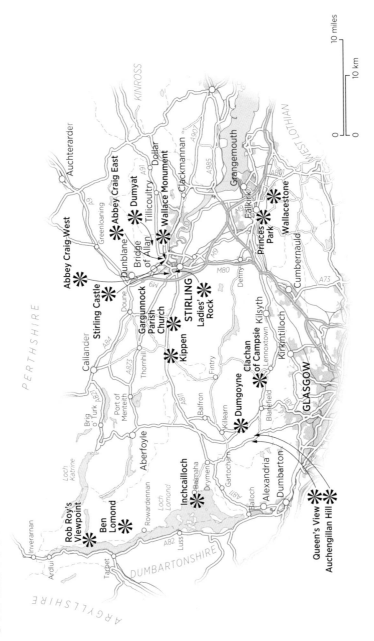

# STIRLINGSHIRE

## Rob Roy's Viewpoint

NN 345 089

Brass disc set on a rock. Erected by 53 Squadron (Airfields) RE in 1966. The disc originally stood next to the car park and remained in this position until at least 1991. It has since been moved to a different rock about 200 yards south. This probably accounts for the slight discrepancy in the position of the viewpoint symbol on Ordnance Survey maps: the *Landranger* shows the old location; the *Explorer* shows the new one. Ben Lomond is not visible, the line of sight being blocked by Cruachan 1762 feet.

> 'Inversnaid car park & picnic area', hand-drawn sketch of the car park area and face of the indicator by T.D. dated 1991, in the records of the Loch Lomond & Trossachs National Park Authority (supplied by Douglas Stewart, 29 April 2009)
>
> 'Looking at Mountain indicator, Inversnaid', photo by KC2000 on Flickr, dated 1967

## Ben Lomond

NN 367 028

Paper chart in glass frame, set on a stone cube. Designed by Duncan K. Paterson, assisted by Tom S. Hall, and erected by the Glasgow and West of Scotland Ramblers' Federation and the *Daily Record*. The Ben Lomond indicator was unveiled on Monday, 1 April 1929 in the presence of around 2000 climbers. It was a compass design with arrows to the features visible. On 9 September 1933, a new chart was installed: etched copper, chromium plated and covered with plate glass. This new chart (also by Paterson) added to the original design an outline of hills based on infra-red photographs taken from the summit by James Duncan of Paisley. The hill identifications were checked by John Mathieson.

Humble in September 1938 found the glass removed, but the plate 'in splendid condition'. Over the next twenty years, the condition of the indicator deteriorated. Around 1960 the plate was stolen leaving only a rusty metal table with four legs (the plinth was originally built round a metal frame).

In August 1962 there was an attempt to install a new indicator at the summit following the donation of a bronze disc by W.R. Millar, a 65-year old retired Edinburgh businessman. The donor set off up the hill with the disc in a rucksack, and R.A.F. Leuchars mountain rescue men carried granite blocks up the lower slopes using a motor cycle, but the attempt was defeated by the weather amid chaotic scenes.

*The Indicator on Ben Lomond. Source: B.H. Humble,* Evening Times, *3 September 1938.*

The rusty metal table survived until at least 23 September 1973 but has since been removed by the National Trust for Scotland on the grounds of health and safety. By the time I climbed Ben Lomond, on 21 December 2007, there was no physical evidence that an indicator had ever stood on the summit.

*The Daily Record Mountain View Indicator on Ben Lomond*, published by Glasgow and West of Scotland Federation of Ramblers (copy of 1929 chart)

'Rowardennan's Greatest Day; Ben Lomond Scenes: 2000 Ben Lomond Climbers', *Daily Record*, 2 April 1929

Tom S. Hall, *Tramping Holidays in Scotland*, 1933, pp.115–118 (see also illustrations facing pages 56 and 116)

'The New Ben Lomond Indicator', *The Scottish Ramblers' Year Book*, 1934, p.9

B.H. Humble, 'The Majesty of Ben Lomond', *Evening Times*, 3 September 1938

'Weather Beats View Indicator Builders: Stone and Cement Lost', *Glasgow Herald*, 6 August 1962

*The Scots Magazine*, Volume 83, Number 2, May 1965, p.188

J.E.R. Squires unpublished hill diary, 23 September 1973

# Dumyat                                           NS 835 976

A carved oak panel in a bronze case with a brass top mounted on a concrete pillar. The wood was carved by Mr. James Scott with paintings by Miss Crum. Erected by Major Frederick Crum and the Scouts of Menstrie, Alva and Stirling in honour of the accession of King Edward VIII. It was unveiled on Saturday, 31 October 1936. Humble reported in an article in the *Evening Times* of 9 July 1938 that the panel was missing and that only the pedestal remained. A hand-written note by Frederick Crum on B.H. Humble's copy of the booklet *The Story of The Dumyat*

*Cairn and Indicator* reads: 'Dear Sir, I have just read your article in Evening Times of July 9th 38 – Alas the indicator was smashed by hooligans & is now in Scout Hall Queen St. Stirling. 14.7.38'. Today, there is no obvious physical evidence even of the pillar on which the oak panel was mounted.

The Story of the Dumyat Cairn and Indicator, undated pamphlet (includes pictures of the oak panel and unveiling ceremony)

*The short-lived Dumyat indicator. Source:* The Story of the Dumyat Cairn and Indicator.

B.H. Humble, 'Western Sentinel of the Ochils: Dumyat, Tillicoultry, and Ben Cleuch', *Evening Times*, 9 July 1938

## Abbey Craig East

NS 810 958

Metal plate on a stone plinth. Erected by Stirling District Council in 1982. The site is called the Ochils Viewpoint on the map of the Abbey Craig available at the nearby Visitor Centre. Myreton Hill is misidentified.

## Wallace Monument

NS 809 956

Four paper charts mounted inside the crown at the top of the Wallace Monument. *The Scotsman* for 1 September 1894 reported that 'four indicator maps' by James Shearer of Stirling had been placed 'on the very top of the monument'. These were surely a version of the 7 foot 3 inch printed panorama by Shearer published in the same year. However, while the published panorama is black and white, the charts on display inside the crown were (at least by the late thirties) coloured. Thus Humble in 1939 reported: 'The four-section view indicator is a coloured outline drawing and one of the best I have seen.' The original charts have been replaced by four plastic panels with a labelled drawing of the view. Access to the crown is by means of a sequence of spiral staircases. The monument is open all year, but there is an admission charge.

'The Wallace Monument', *The Scotsman*, 1 September 1894

James E. Shearer, *Panorama seen from the National Wallace Monument, Abbey Craig, Stirling* (7 ft 3 inches x 5¾ inches). Stirling: R.S. Shearer and Son, 1894.

Ben Humble, 'What is Scotland's Finest View?', *SMT Magazine*, September 1939

# Abbey Craig West    NS 809 956

Metal plate on a stone plinth. Erected by Stirling District Council in 1992. One of a pair with Abbey Craig East in terms of the style of the plate, although the stone work of the plinth here is more formal. It will be found about 20 yards west of the Wallace Monument.

# Kippen   NS 647 945

Metal plate, about 4½ feet long by 10 inches wide, on metal legs. Erected by Kippen Community Council in 1996. The design of the plate was based on a panorama by Buchanan, published more than sixty years earlier. Four of the twenty or so peaks are misidentified.

> D. Buchanan, *Panorama view from Kippen*. Stirling: Jamieson & Munro, 1930.
>
> Personal communication, Fiona Clark, Kippen Community Council, 16 April 2010

*Plate mounted at Kippen. Photo taken 11/03/2010.*

# Gargunnock Parish Church   NS 707 943

Bronze plate on the north-facing balcony of a church. The plate carries the words

'In Memoriam John Stirling Stirling & Charles Stirling' and the date 1960. There are also six sets of initials. Local historian John McLaren has identified VHCS as Viola Henrietta Christian Stirling (1907–1989), but is unsure about the other five. Among the unidentified is the designer of the plate, DWS. McLaren believes that it was originally intended to mount the plate on a plinth at the top of the village, opposite the house called Carseview, on the grounds that only from there could most of the depicted view be seen. In its current site on the balcony wall of the church, it is reached by a stone staircase.

*Gargunnock News*, Spring 2007, pp.14–15

Personal communication, John McLaren, 17 December 2009

# Stirling Castle                                                   NS 790 939

Four panels on the parapet of a twelfth century castle. The panels are titled:

1. The Populated Lowlands (NS 790 939), which looks south-east from the wall of the outer defences of the castle.
2. The Ochil Fault (NS 790 940), which looks north from the Grand Battery. This panel is becoming difficult to read.
3. Birthplace of a Nation (NS 789 940), which looks south-west from the Ladies' Lookout.
4. Lava Flows and Raised Beaches (NS 789 940), which looks west from the Ladies' Lookout.

The panels were installed by Historic Scotland in the 1990s. On panel 4, the peak identified as Ben Ledi is Beinn Narnain.

The castle is open daily throughout the year; there is a charge for admission.

Personal communication, Kit Reid, Historic Scotland

# Ladies' Rock                                                      NS 791 937

Circular paper chart in a glass frame mounted on a stone plinth. Designed by James Shearer, erected by Stirling Town Council and unveiled on Monday, 11 August 1890. Shearer's circular chart survived until at least June 1938, but has since been replaced by a bronze disc of different design. The only known images of the original chart are in *Stirling: Gateway To The Highlands*, a silent black-and-white tourist film produced by Stirling Council c.1938. The chart showed local landmarks such as Stirling Castle and the Wallace Monument around the edge. Separately, in a rectangular strip in the middle was a labelled outline of the western Grampians. Some five years after the indicator was installed, the artist Arthur Harris published a panorama drawn from Ladies' Rock.

> Minutes of Provost's Committee of Stirling Town Council for 21 April, 16 and 19 May, 11 and 18 August, 1890
>
> 'Indicator on the Ladies' Rock, Stirling', *Stirling Observer*, 13 August 1890
>
> 'The Indicator for the Ladies' Rock', *Stirling Journal & Advertiser*, 15 August 1890
>
> Arthur Harris, *The Stirling Panorama from the Ladies Rock* (8ft 6 inches x 9¼ inches). Stirling: Eneas Mackay, 1895.
>
> B.H. Humble, 'What Stirling Has to Give', *Evening Times*, 25 June 1938

*The indicator on the Ladies' Rock at Stirling, dating from 1890, was the first to be installed in Scotland (and so far as I am aware, in Britain). Originally the plinth was topped by a glass-covered paper chart. Photo taken 18/05/2009.*

## Inchcailloch

NS 410 903

Aluminium plate on a metal stand. Erected by the Nature Conservancy Council, probably c.1968 in connection with a nature trail set up on the island at that time. A photograph in Pennyfather's *Guide* shows that it was in place by 1975. The aluminium plate carried a photograph which identified features in the view northwards to the head of Loch Lomond. Sometime in the 1990s, Scottish Natural Heritage replaced the original indicator with one of a different design. This consisted of a metal plate with a labelled drawing of the view, mounted on metal legs embedded in a stone cairn. About 2007, SNH and Loch Lomond and the Trossachs National Park decided to remove this device. When I visited on 11 March 2010, there was no physical evidence that an indicator had ever stood here.

Keith Pennyfather, *Guide to Countryside Interpretation: part two*, 1975 p.89 and Plate 39

'Inchcailloch Island Camping Loch Lomond', YouTube video from 2005 uploaded by Nabrach (includes footage of the SNH replacement)

Personal communication, Tim Jacobs, SNH, 30 April 2009

## Dumgoyne                                               NS 541 827

Metal disc set on a stone. Erected by Strathendrick Rotarians. The stone was installed on an octagonal concrete base, using a helicopter, on 31 May 2000. The metal disc followed in June. By September 2000, the disc had been removed. It was still missing when I visited on 11 March 2010. The stone and the concrete base remained.

'Late News: Dumgoyne', *The Angry Corrie* 46, July-Aug 2000

'Roll Away the Stone', *The Angry Corrie* 48, Jan-Feb 2001

## Queen's View, Auchineden                               NS 510 807

Steel plate on a plinth of local stone. Erected by the Automobile Association and unveiled on Tuesday, 2 June 1964. When I visited on 16 May 2009, the plate was missing. The plinth remained.

'Scotland's "rest and view" sites', *Evening Times*, 2 June 1964

'Loch Lomond Viewpoint for Tourists', *The Glasgow Herald*, 3 June 1964

'Point of View', *Country Life*, 2 July 1964, p.22

## Auchengillan Hill                                       NS 515 806

Copper disc, chromium plated and covered with glass, on a stone cairn. Designed by Duncan K. Paterson and presented by the *Daily Record* to the Glasgow Boy Scouts. It was unveiled on Sunday, 26 June 1932 in a ceremony 'witnessed by hundreds of Rovers, in their kilts and Balmorals, Scouts and members of the

*Derelict Automobile Association indicator at Queen's View,*
*Auchineden. Photo taken 16/05/2009.*

public'. One of a pair with the Everton Park indicator, the plate was engraved
with the Scout Badge in the centre and had a labelled outline of mountains
around the edge. Humble in 1938 found the disc 'more badly scratched than
any other indicator I have seen' and the chromium plating starting to peel off. By
1979, one section of the disc was missing and the cairn was disintegrating. When
I visited on 23 April 2010, the only physical remains were the concrete base on

which the cairn stood. Coniferous trees planted by the Scouts over a period of years, principally the 1950s, completely blocked the view.

'Guide to Panorama of Mountain Peaks', *Daily Record*, 27 June 1932

Tom S. Hall, 'Lomond View Indicator', *Citizen Rambles: Byways and Uplands*, p.15

B.H. Humble, 'Glasgow Scouts are Lucky', *Evening Times*, 17 September 1938

Personal communications, Andy Wilson, Auchengillan Outdoor Centre, 8 June 2009 and 6 March 2010

## Clachan of Campsie                                                    NS 610 795

Square panel on a stone cairn. Erected by Fells View Training with funding from East Dunbartonshire Council. A tribute to the climber and broadcaster Tom Weir, it was unveiled in September 2004 in his presence. The idea of the cairn originated with Betty Gorman of the Strathkelvin Ramblers. It has been sited behind conifers which block the view even in mid-winter. Mark Brand tells me that the council and Strathkelvin Ramblers had hoped for a more open position for the cairn, but this was vetoed by the landowner.

Confusingly, the photograph on the panel was taken from the other side of the valley and not from Clachan of Campsie.

'Weir the walking people', *Lennoxtown Initiative Newsletter*, issue 4, January 2005

Personal communication, Mark Brand, East Dunbartonshire Council, 4 February 2011

## Princes Park                                                          NS 879 788

Copper half-disc, chromium plated and covered with glass, on a stone cairn. Designed by Duncan K. Paterson with assistance from Tom S. Hall and presented by the *Daily Record* to Falkirk Town Council. A crowd of 50 or 60 mackintosh-clad spectators braved miserable weather to attend the unveiling ceremony on Saturday, 14 September 1935. The plate was removed for security reasons during the Second World War, but was returned to the plinth c.1947. The original metal plate has been replaced by a paper chart of similar design, marked 'Drawn by D.K. Paterson, Revised by J.R. Palmer 1982'. Photographs of the original exist in the Falkirk Council archive.

The peak identified as Meall Gruaidh (now called Meall Greigh 1001m on Ordnance Survey maps) is Creag Uchdag 879m; the peak identified as Skythorn is Andrew Gannel Hill 670m. Another doubtful point relates to Ben Chonzie

931m. The chart states that the peak is not visible; digital models suggest that a small portion can be seen.

Separate from the Princes Park chart, D. K. Paterson drew an outline of the horizon as seen from the west end of Wester Shieldhill, 2½ miles south of Falkirk.

Falkirk Town Council Minutes, 10 December 1934

*The Princes Park View Indicator*, printed copy of the original chart

'New View Indicator for Falkirk', *Daily Record*, 16 September 1935

'Mountain View Indicator Handed Over', *Falkirk Herald*, 18 September 1935

'Gift to the Town', *Falkirk Mail*, 20 September 1935

D.K. Paterson (revised by D. Ferguson, A.M.I.C.E) *Outline of the Horizon as seen from west end of Wester Shieldhill, 680 feet high and 2½ miles south of Falkirk.* Undated item, reference A558.063, held in the Falkirk Council Archive.

Tom S. Hall, *Country Walks in Scotland,* undated, c.1947, Introduction

## Wallacestone                                                   NS 918 770

Metal disc, covered with plastic, on a stone cylinder. The disc carries no information as to the installer or date and enquiries to Falkirk Council and the local community council did not prove fruitful.

# CLACKMANNANSHIRE

PERTHSHIRE

KINROSS

Dunblane

Glendevon

A823

Glendevon
Reservoirs

Yetts o'
Muckhart

A91

Dollar

Castle
Campbell ✳

Ben
Cleuch ✳

Tillicoultry
Hill ✳

Tillicoultry ✳

A91

A823

Bridge
of Allan

A9

Menstrie  Alva  Tillicoultry

A91

Sauchie

A91

Gartmorn
Reservoir

Gartmorn Dam ✳

Clackmannan

A907

A907

A985

Kincardine

Tullibody

Alloa

River Forth

Airth

A905

STIRLING

Bannockburn

Cowie

M9

M9

STIRLINGSHIRE

0 —— 10 km

0 —— 10 miles

# CLACKMANNANSHIRE

## Ben Cleuch

NN 902 006

Paper chart in a glass frame, set on a stone cube. Designed by Duncan K. Paterson, with the assistance of Tom S. Hall, and erected by Tillicoultry Town Council. The Ben Cleuch view indicator, which was a gift of the *Daily Record*, was unveiled by James A. Parker on Saturday, 14 June 1930 in the presence of a crowd 'numbering close on a thousand'. The paper original was replaced with a chromium-plated copper plate in 1934. This was removed from the plinth for security reasons during the Second World War but reinstated c.1947. The plate was again removed from the summit between May 1988 and May 1990 for restoration, a project involving Venture Scouts from Clackmannan and Jamieson-MacGregor Ltd, Engineers. It was in serviceable condition when I visited on 10 March 2010. James Gardner, one of the officers of the Ordnance Survey who was stationed on Ben Cleuch in the nineteenth century, published a beautiful folding panorama of the view.

Beinn a'Bhuird 1197m and Mount Keen 939m are not visible. Cairn Toul 1291m is marginal.

James Gardner, *A View of the Grampian Mountains from the Summit of Benclach* (6 ft 3 inches x 11 inches). London: James Gardner, 1820 (another edition was published by J.A. Knipe in 1875)

Alexander Ross Clarke, *Account of the Observations and Calculations of the Principal Triangulation*, 1858, p.78

*The Ben Cleuch Mountain View Indicator*, undated pamphlet with printed copy of the original chart

'Ben Cleuch View Indicator', *Daily Record*, 14 June 1930

'Daily Record View Indicator Inaugurated on Ben Cleuch', *Daily Record*, 16 June 1930

'Indicator on Ben Cleuch', *The Scotsman*, 16 June 1930

J. A. Parker, 'The Tinto Indicator', *Cairngorm Club Journal*, Volume 14, number 77, June 1936, pp.110–114

'Mountain Vistas', letter from the Provost of Tillicoultry, *The Scotsman*, 18 October 1946

*Inauguration of the* Daily Record *view indicator on Ben Cleuch. J. A. Parker, who performed the ceremony, is the bearded man standing behind the plinth. Source:* Daily Record *16 June 1930.*

# Castle Campbell

NS 961 992

Laminated chart mounted on the parapet of a fifteenth century tower. Erected by Historic Scotland in the late 1990s. Access is by means of a spiral staircase. The castle is open throughout the year; there is an admission charge.

Personal communication, Kit Reid, Historic Scotland

*A panel at Castle Campbell describes the view over the valley of the River Forth. Photo taken 16/03/2011.*

# Tillicoultry Hill                                    NS 913 978

Zinc plate in a glass frame, mounted on a wooden stand. Designed by the architect Arthur Bracewell, erected by Tillicoultry Town Council and unveiled on Saturday, 31 August 1929. The indicator was a gift of 'Tillyonians in Toronto' to the council, and was part of a scheme directed by Bracewell to open up Tillicoultry Glen through a system of paths and bridges. An evocative photograph of this indicator, taken in 1962 when it was still intact, has been posted on Geograph. When I visited the site on 10 March 2010, all that remained was the concrete base on which it stood, with three bolts and a scrap of wood.

'Indicator on Tillicoultry Hill', *The Scotsman*, 2 September 1929

B.H. Humble, *Wayfaring Around Scotland*, 1936, p.200

'Above the Quarry', photo dated 1962 by James Allan, on Geograph

# Gartmorn Dam                                         NS 920 936

Bronze disc on a stone cylinder. Erected by Clackmannanshire Riders Access Group to commemorate Queen Elizabeth's Golden Jubilee in June 2002. The bronze disc has been missing for several years; the landowner tells me there are no plans to install a new one. The stone cylinder remains.

Personal communication, Jane Coull, 27 September 2013

# KINROSS

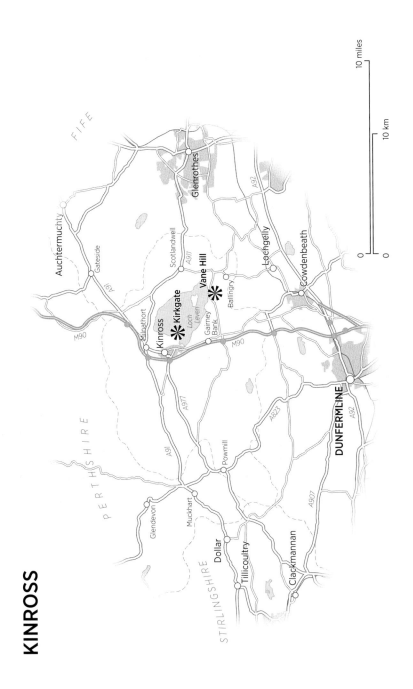

# Kinross-shire

## Kirkgate

NO 128 017

A curved metal bar, perhaps 30 feet long, mounted on seven metal struts. The metal bar carries drawings of the hills to the east, as well as the local wildlife. Designed by the artist David Wilson and erected by TRACKS (The Rural Access Committee for Kinross-shire) in 2008.

*Kinross Newsletter*, Issue 354, July 2008, p.9

*The Kirkgate viewpoint, on the western shore of Loch Leven. Photo taken 25/04/2010.*

## Vane Hill

NT 163 989

Hamish Brown mentions a viewpoint indicator at this site in a 1995 guidebook. It is most likely that it was installed by the RSPB some time after they acquired Vane Farm in 1967. The RPSB confirmed that there was at one time an indicator at this site, but did not know whether they had installed it, when it had been installed or when it was removed. By the time I visited, on 6 December 2009, there was no physical evidence that an indicator had ever stood here. The site is marked by a viewpoint symbol on some old Ordnance Survey maps.

Hamish Brown, *Fife: 25 Walks*, 1995, p.23

# FIFE

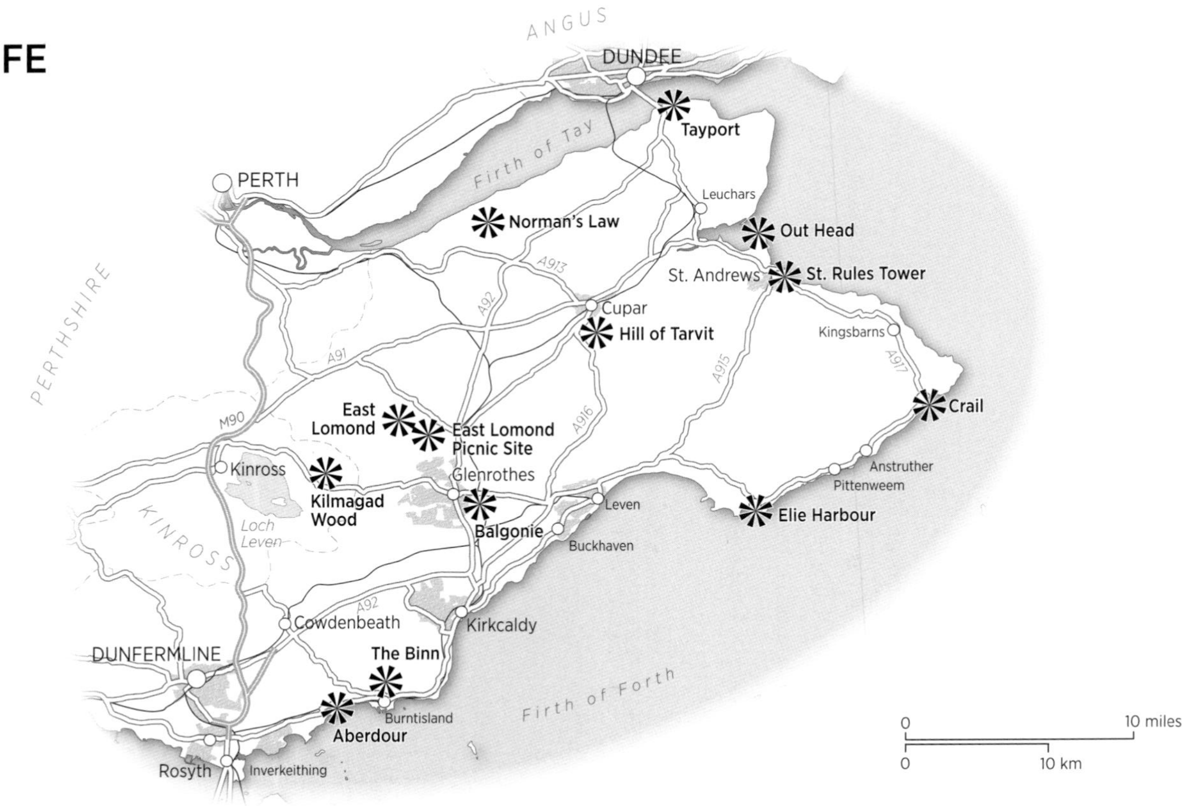

PERTH

DUNDEE

ANGUS

PERTHSHIRE

KINROSS

Firth of Tay

Firth of Forth

Tayport

Norman's Law

Leuchars

Out Head

St. Andrews

St. Rules Tower

Kingsbarns

Crail

Anstruther

Pittenweem

Elie Harbour

A917

A915

Cupar

Hill of Tarvit

A916

A92

A913

Leven

Buckhaven

Balgonie

Glenrothes

East Lomond
Picnic Site

East
Lomond

Kilmagad
Wood

Kinross

Loch
Leven

M90

A91

Kirkcaldy

The Binn

Cowdenbeath

Burntisland

Aberdour

A92

DUNFERMLINE

Rosyth

Inverkeithing

10 miles

10 km

0

0

# Fife

## Tayport
NO 435 290

Metal plate in three sections, mounted on wooden posts. Designed by Connon Design Associates and installed by Scottish Water on completion of the nearby waste water treatment plant, c.2006.

## Norman's Law
NO 305 202

Metal plate on a stone plinth. Erected by the friends of Duncan Wilson (1937–1992) as a memorial. It was in place by 1997.

Record for Normans Law on Trigpointinguk

## Out Head
NO 494 196

Laminated panel, about 7½ feet by 15 inches, mounted on a wooden viewing platform. Erected by Fife Coast and Countryside Trust in 2010. The peak identified as Dundee Law is something else. Dundee Law would appear to the west of the high point of the Sidlaws and not the east as shown.

Fife Environment Trust Newsletter 2010, Issue 11

## St. Rules Tower
NO 514 166

Laminated panel on the parapet of a twelfth century tower. Erected by Historic Scotland. The date is uncertain. Kit Reid suggested that the panel was installed in the mid-1990s, but it was not present when I visited the tower on 26 October 1998. The parapet is reached by a spiral staircase inside the tower, which is open throughout the year. There is a charge for admission.

Personal communication, Kit Reid, Historic Scotland, 6 January 2011

*Panel on the parapet of St.Rules Tower, St.Andrews. Photo taken 16/03/2011.*

# Hill of Tarvit                    NO 375 120

Four metal plates, one for each point of the compass, mounted almost at ground level on concrete supports. Erected by the National Trust for Scotland in 1980. The metal plates, which are each about a yard from the base of a nineteenth century stone monument, carry labelled photographs. Five features are misidentified, most notably Norman's Law.

# Crail                                                      NO 613 074

Framed paper chart. Erected by the Crail Preservation Society in 2007. The chart is mounted on railings, a few yards from an old stone sundial on the Castle Promenade.

# East Lomond                                                NO 244 061

Bronze disc on a granite column. Designed by John Mathieson, donated by Mary and Agnes Lumsden and unveiled on Saturday, 6 October 1928. About the year 2000, the disc went missing and was replaced by one designed by Jonathan de Ferranti. However, the original disc was recovered and had been re-attached to the plinth by September 2004.

Five years before Mathieson's disc was installed, John S. Ramsay published a panorama drawn from the summit.

*Unveiling the indicator on East Lomond, 6 October 1928. The donors Mary and Agnes Lumsden are at the extreme left and right of the picture. The gentleman furthest to the right is (I believe) the designer, John Mathieson. Source: Fife News Almanac 1929*

John S. Ramsay, *Panorama seen from Falkland Hill, East Lomond*. Kirkcaldy: The Fifeshire Advertiser Ltd, 1923

'Falkland Hill Panorama', *Cairngorm Club Journal*, Volume 11, issue 61, p.47, July 1923

'Mountain Indicator: East Lomond Ceremony', *The Scotsman*, 8 October 1928 (mildly amusing corrigendum 10 October)

'Hill Indicator Unveiled on East Lomond', *Fife News*, 13 October 1928

'Geographical Indicator on East Lomond, Fife', *Scottish Geographical Magazine*, Volume 44, issue 6, 1928, pp.361–362

Personal communication, Jonathan de Ferranti, 14 September 2004

# East Lomond Picnic Site                                    NO 252 058

Metal plate, covered with perspex, on a stone plinth. Erected by Fife Regional Council in 1986 to mark the creation of the Fife Regional Park (now known as the Lomond Hills Regional Park).

'The Lomonds' Proposed Regional Park, Countryside Grant Application, D5/C2/42, undated document in Fife Council Archive (includes architectural drawings of indicator)

# Kilmagad Wood

NO 186 021

Laminated panel, about 55 inches by 18, mounted on oak timbers. Erected by the Woodland Trust in the autumn of 2012.

Personal communication, Gary Bolton, Woodland Trust, 7 January 2013.

*A view from Kilmagad Wood, overlooking Loch Leven. Photo taken 25/05/2013.*

# Balgonie

NO 302 006

Laminated disc on a dressed stone cairn. Erected by Milton & Coaltown of Balgonie Community Council in 2008. The orientation of the disc is so poor that the device is practically useless.

Personal communication, Alistair Milligan, 7 January 2010

# Elie Harbour

NT 492 995

Metal disc on a stone cylinder. Designed by Jeremy Eccles and erected by Elie Harbour Trust in 1993. If you are using Ordnance Survey maps to find this indicator, beware of the discrepancy between the *Landranger* and *Explorer*. The position of the indicator corresponds to the viewpoint on the *Explorer*.

*Viewpoint at Elie Harbour. Photo taken 23/08/2009.*

## The Binn                                                          NT 235 869

Metal disc on a stone cylinder. Erected by Burntisland and Kinghorn Rotary Club in 1992.

## Aberdour                                                          NT 201 857

Framed paper chart, about 25 inches square, on a stone plinth. Erected by Fife Council around 14 July 2010. The peaks identified as Meikle Says Law 535m, East Cairn Hill 567m and Black Hill 501m are all other objects.

> 'Aberdour Viewpoint Interpretation Panel Unveiled', Fife Council news release published on Wednesday 14 July 2010.

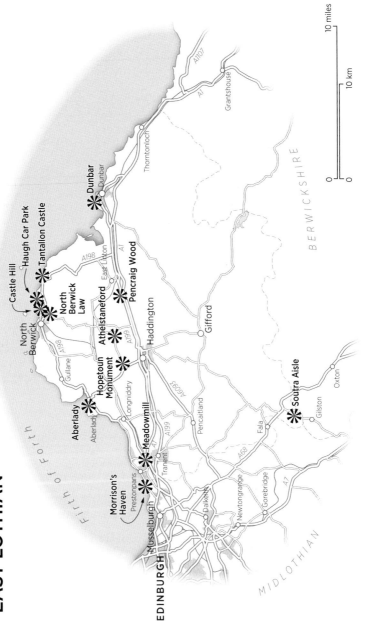

# EAST LOTHIAN

# East Lothian

## Haugh Car Park  NT 568 852

Framed paper chart on a stone cairn. Erected by North Berwick Environment Trust in partnership with East Lothian Council. Enquiries to these organisations yielded no definite information as to designer or date. It is most likely that the device was installed in the early 2000s, as there is a viewpoint symbol at this location on the 2003 edition of the Ordnance Survey map *Southern Scotland & Northumberland*, but not the 1999 edition.

## Castle Hill  NT 560 851

Framed paper chart, about 52 inches by 25, mounted on wooden legs. Erected by East Lothian Council and the Friends of the Law & Glen (FLAG) in 2007, and renewed in 2012. The feature identified as the Lomond Hills is Largo Law.

Personal communication, Renate Gertz, East Lothian Council 21 October 2013

## Tantallon Castle  NT 595 850

Two panels mounted on the tower of a fourteenth century castle. Erected by Historic Scotland in the mid-1990s. One panel looks south and the other west. The panels are reached by a spiral staircase. The castle opens daily throughout the year; there is a charge for admission.

Personal communication, Kit Reid, Historic Scotland.

## North Berwick Law  NT 556 842

Bronze plate on a dressed stone cylinder. Designed by John C. Bartholomew and erected in 1959 as a memorial to John Wallace Menzies (1889–1956), solicitor and town clerk of North Berwick. The device stands on a cobbled octagonal base.

*The summit of North Berwick Law. Photo taken 02/12/2009.*

# Aberlady
NT 464 801

Printed chart, covered with plastic, on metal legs. Designed by Sean Trevarthen and erected c.2000. There were originally two charts on either side of a telescope. The charts remain but the telescope has disappeared.

Personal communication, Sean Trevarthen, 27 December 2010

# Dunbar
NT 671 793

Metal disc, about three feet across, on a cone of concrete. Enquiries yielded no definite information as to who installed this device or its date. It is marked on the 1964 edition of 1:2,500 scale Ordnance Survey map as a 'Tablet'. Allister Combe, a former Dunbar resident, remembers the disc as being in position in 1980. When I visited, on 2 December 2009, it was missing. The concrete cone remained.

Personal communication, Stephen Bunyan, Dunbar Community Council, 12 December 2009 and Allister Combe, 1 May 2009

*Derelict view indicator at Dunbar. Photo taken 02/12/2009.*

# Athelstaneford
NT 532 773

Panel mounted on a wooden post. Erected by the Scottish Flag Trust, and opened by Dr Winnie Ewing MSP on Friday, 27 April 2001. It will be found a few yards from a doocot located on the north side of the church.

*The Athelstaneford Saltire: Newsletter of the Scottish Flag Trust*, No. 5, June 2001

# Pencraig Wood
NT 573 765

Three melamine panels set on the wall of a stone viewing platform. Erected by East Lothian Council and opened on Tuesday, 7 July 1970. Access to the viewing platform is by steps. The original panels, designed by Russell Turner, have been replaced.

'Pencraik Hill Picnic Site Inspected', *The Haddingtonshire Courier*, 10 July 1970

Don Aldridge, *Guide to Countryside Interpretation: part one*, 1975, plate 98

Frank Tindall, *Memoirs & Confessions of a County Planning Officer*, 1998, pp.240–242

## Hopetoun Monument                                     NT 500 764

Twelve panels, each about 22 inches by 10 inches, set around the parapet of a
nineteenth century tower. Drawn by the graphic designer Margaret Montgomery,
the panels were installed by East Lothian Council c.1983 and renewed in the
1990s. The parapet is reached by means of a dark, crumbling spiral staircase inside
the tower. It is not recommended to those who suffer from vertigo.

> Countryside Commission for Scotland, *Sixteenth Report*, 1983, p.40
>
> Personal communication, Duncan Priddle, East Lothian Council, 16 December
> 2009

## Meadowmill                                            NT 401 739

Eight metal panels on a metal stand. Designed by Margaret Montgomery and
erected by East Lothian District Council in 1975. The panels stand on a grassy
pyramid originally sculpted from a coal bing.

> Frank Tindall, *Memoirs & Confessions of a County Planning Officer*, 1998, p.15
>
> 'A Victory Salute', *The Scotsman*, 18 September 2008

## Morrison's Haven                                      NT 370 737

Three laminated panels set on a curved stone wall. Erected by East Lothian
Council in 1995/96. The Cleish Hills and the Pentlands are misidentified.

> Personal communication, Sarah Cheyne, East Lothian Council, 31 March 2010

## Soutra Aisle                                          NT 452 584

Six panels set into an octagonal stone a few yards away from the remains of
a twelfth century hospital. Three of the panels carry a labelled drawing due to
Alistair Chisholm. This was based on a hand-drawn panorama by Chris Jesty and
a digital panorama by Jonathan de Ferranti. Erected by Fala, Soutra & District
History & Heritage Society, and unveiled on Saturday, 1 May 1999. The text on
the panels was due to Dr. Brian Moffat. One of them states that 'In guidebooks it
is rightly called *the finest view in Southern Scotland*'. In response to an enquiry as to
which guidebooks he had in mind, Dr. Moffat referred to Pennant, the Baedeker
and Blue Guides but explained that the claim 'is not made explicit'. Indeed,
the claim is not made at all. The strongest praise in any of these guidebooks is
Pennant's assertion that it is 'a fine view'.

Chris Jesty, *Panorama from Soutra Hill.* (16½" by 8"), Bridport: Jesty's Panoramas.

Jonathan de Ferranti, *Soutra Aisle* (digital panorama), 1995

Personal communication, Dr. Brain Moffat, SHARP

'Soutra opens as a tourist attraction', *East Lothian Courier*, 7 May 1999

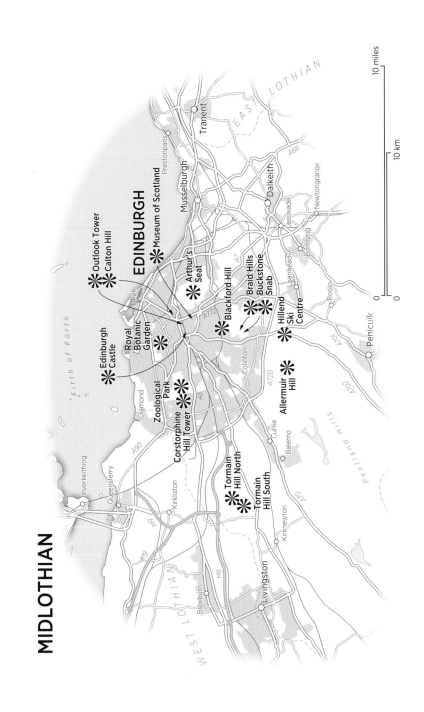

# Midlothian

## Royal Botanic Garden

NT 245 752

A framed panel, 7½ feet long by 12 inches deep, mounted at eye-level on three legs. Erected by H.M. Office of Works c.1921, the panel carried an image assembled from photographs by Robert M. Adam and a labelled sketch. It was the gift of William Mair (1868–1948), chemist and historian of Morningside. The panel was located about 100 yards from Inverleith House at the 'City View Point' which is marked in several editions of the official guide to the Garden. The four photographs from which the panel was made are dated 10 June 1921 in Adam's register in the Garden's archive.

A photograph in the RCAHMS archive shows that by 1986, the original panel had been replaced by one of different design. This took the form of a drawing mounted at waist height on two legs. By the time I visited, on 4 December 2009, this had been removed and there was no physical evidence that an indicator ever stood here.

> *The Royal Botanic Garden: A Brief Descriptive and Illustrated Account*, Edinburgh: His Majesty's Stationery Office, 1934 (the image and sketch which appeared on the panel is at pp.36–37; there is also a map showing the position of the 'City View Point')
>
> 'Men and women of today', *The Courier and Advertiser*, 4 February 1937
>
> B.H. Humble, 'What is Scotland's Finest View?', *SMT Magazine*, September 1939, pp.50–52 (photo of the original indicator)
>
> Item A66095/17CN in RCAHMS archive
>
> Personal communication, Leonie Paterson, Archives Librarian, Royal Botanic Garden, 3 November 2009

## Calton Hill

NT 262 742

Laminated panel, titled 'All along the Firth of Forth', mounted on two metal legs. Designed by Studioarc and erected by Edinburgh City Council in 2009. The location is called the 'North Viewpoint' on maps displayed in Calton Hill public park.

> Personal communication Sue Brown, Edinburgh City Council, 21 January 2013

# Corstorphine Hill NT 206 738

Two bronze plates set on the pigeon turret of a nineteenth century tower. Designed by John Mathieson and installed by Edinburgh City Corporation around 11 December 1933. The plates were the gift of James Duke Monro, a retired tea merchant who was also a trustee of the Royal Scottish Geographical Society. Access is by means of a spiral staircase. At present, the tower is only open on Sunday afternoons between May and September (see the website of the Friends of Corstorphine Hill for details). An admission charge is made. At least four peaks on the plates are not visible: Blackhope Scar, Earl's Seat, Ben Lawers and Dun Rig.

'Indicator on Corstorphine Hill', *The Scotsman*, 11 December 1933

# Edinburgh Castle NT 251 735

Two oval charts mounted on the parapet of a castle. One is titled 'The View North over the City' and has been mounted at a point called 'North Panorama', among the cannons of the Argyll Battery. The other is titled 'The View West over the City' and has been mounted at a point called 'West Panorama' (NT 250 735). The charts were erected by Historic Scotland in the early 1990s. The castle opens daily throughout the year. There is an admission charge.

Personal communication, Kit Reid, Historic Scotland

# Zoological Park NT 209 735

Bronze disc on a dressed stone cylinder. Designed by John Mathieson and erected by Edinburgh Zoological Garden in September 1938. The indicator was funded by a bequest made by Charles J.G. Paterson of Castle Huntly, who had died the previous year. The cylinder is set on a circular paved area surrounded by railings. Edinburgh Zoo is open all year but there is an admission charge.

# Outlook Tower NT 254 735

About 35 arrows cut into the stone parapet of a nineteenth century tower. The arrows were cut c.1894 on the initiative of Professor Patrick Geddes, at that time the tower's owner. They were oriented by the French geographer and anarchist Élisée Reclus. Geddes was a charismatic educationalist who used the tower as a venue for a geographic exhibition. Today, the tower is operated as the 'Camera Obscura and World of Illusions'. A number of alterations have been made since

*Indicator at Edinburgh Zoo. Photo taken 09/05/2010.*

Geddes owned the tower. Railings have been installed on the parapet, damaging the engraved arrows, and three metal panels with labelled drawings of the view have been attached to the railings. Telescopes have also been added. Access to the parapet is by means of stairs inside the tower, which is open all year. There is an admission charge.

Most of the arrows point to towns, but directions are also given for Ben Lomond and the Isle of May, which are visible (at least in a digital world without buildings).

William Mair 'Scottish View Indicators and Panoramas', *Scottish Geographical Magazine*, Volume 55, issue 2, 1939, pp.102–107

# Museum of Scotland                            NT 257 732

Four panels installed on the roof terrace of a museum. Erected by National Museums Scotland in 2005. The panels show the view to the north, north-east, west and south. Access to the roof terrace is either by lift or a sequence of staircases.

Personal communication, Dawn Lindsay, National Museums Scotland, 25 September 2013

# Arthur's Seat

NT 275 729

Bronze disc on a granite pillar. Designed by John Mathieson and erected by H.M. Office of Works in July 1912. The disc has been renewed several times, most recently with a steel disc which carries a metric version of Mathieson's original design. Chris Jesty published a panorama drawn from Arthur's Seat in 1980.

'Useful Indicator on Arthur's Seat', *Edinburgh Evening News*, 26 July 1912

'Interesting Indicator on Arthur's Seat', *The Scotsman*, 26 July 1912

'Holyrood Park: Arthur's Seat: Erection of a Pedestal Indicator showing outstanding landmarks', Ministry of Works file, PRO reference MW/3/169 in the National Archives of Scotland

Chris Jesty, *Panorama from Arthur's Seat* (2ft 8¼ inches x 9¾ inches). Bridport: Jesty's Panoramas, 1980.

# Blackford Hill

NT 254 706

Metal disc on a stone plinth. Erected by the Automobile Association in 1987. The AA disc was stolen in 2006. A new disc was installed in March 2008 by the Friends of the Hermitage. The replacement names fewer features, but unlike the original has a drawing of the skyline around the edge. The peak identified as Dalmahoy Hill is Warklaw Hill.

'Hill Start', *Glasgow Herald*, 15 June 1987

'P5130113', photo by Catriana McKie, dated 13 May 2006, posted on Flickr (original disc in situ)

*Hill & Hermitage: Newsletter of the Friends of the Hermitage of Braid and Blackford* for December 2007 and March 2008

# Tormain Hill North

NT 129 700

Curved metal plate, about 5 feet long by 11 inches wide, on a metal stand. Erected by the Ratho Environment Group in 2003. The plate looks towards Edinburgh. The feature identified as the Cullaloe Hills is The Binn 191m. The Cullaloe Hills are about ten degrees further west.

Description of 'Tormain Wood Access project' under CERS projects 2002–03 on the Scottish Government website (scotland.gov.uk)

# Tormain Hill South

NT 129 698

One of a pair with Tormain Hill North, but located about 200 yards further south. The plate looks towards the Trossachs and Ochils.

# Braid Hills

NT 249 698

A framed photograph, 6½ feet long by 18 inches deep, mounted on legs at a child's eye-level. More than 50 features were named on the photograph, the identifications being due to John Mathieson. The indicator was erected privately around 28 December 1936 and donated to Edinburgh City Corporation. Like the similar device at the Royal Botanic Garden, it was the gift of William Mair. Its location has been variously described as 'beside the flag-pole behind the original club-house'

*Three schoolchildren examine the Braid Hills indicator. It is no longer extant. Source:* The Scotsman, *16 January 1937.*

and 'on the rocky eminence immediately behind the old golf club house'. In 1988, Charles Smith wrote that 'Mr Mair's interesting and imaginative gift has long since been removed'. When I visited on 3 December 2009, no physical remains could be detected.

*The Scotsman* says that a bronze disc, similar to those that Mathieson designed for Arthur's Seat and Corstorphine Tower, was installed at the same time as the photographic panel. But it is curious that it does not appear in the photographs in *The Scotsman* or Mair's book, and it is not beyond doubt that there was a disc in addition to the panel. Mair lived a few hundred yards away at 32 Braid Hills Road.

'Indicator on Braid Hills', *The Scotsman*, 28 December 1936

'On the Braid Hills', *The Scotsman*, 16 January 1937 (photo of three schoolchildren looking at the panel)

William Mair, *Historic Morningside*, 1947 (includes a fold-out reproduction of the image that was carried on the indicator at a one-third scale)

Charles Smith, *Historic South Edinburgh*, vol. 4, 1988, p.279–281 (biography of Mair)

# Buckstone Snab

NT 248 695

Laminated disc on a red sandstone table. Designed by the cartographer John C. Bartholomew, erected by the City of Edinburgh and unveiled on Wednesday, 5 July 1995.

# Hillend Ski Centre

NT 242 663

Metal half-disc on a stone cairn. A second cairn, a couple of yards from the indicator, used to carry binoculars. It seems most likely that these facilities were installed by Lothian District Council in connection with the construction of the nearby ski-lift, which opened in October 1966. They were certainly in place by 1985. The cairns will be found about 20 yards west of the top station of the ski-lift.

Ben Lawers and Schiehallion are not visible. It is curious that (a) both peaks are visible from the summit of Caerketton Hill about 300 metres away and (b) some old Ordnance Survey maps have a viewpoint symbol there. Perhaps at one stage it was planned to site the indicator at the summit of Caerketton Hill rather than its current position?

Michelin *Scotland*, 1985, p.101

Personal communication, Victor Partridge, Pentland Hills Regional Park, 27 April 2009

# Allermuir Hill

NT 227 662

Metal disc on a stone cylinder. Gifted to the National Trust for Scotland by Arthur Russell and unveiled on Monday, 5 October 1964. Russell was a member of the Scottish Mountaineering Club and the Trust's first Secretary and Treasurer. The Trust renewed the indicator in June 2013. Five peaks are misidentified.

'New landmark in the Pentlands', *The Scotsman*, 6 October 1964

'Arthur W. Russell (1864–1967)', *Scottish Mountaineering Club Journal*, Volume 29, issue 159, May 1968, p. 88

'Midlothian's indicator of trust success', *Midlothian Advertiser*, 23 June 2013

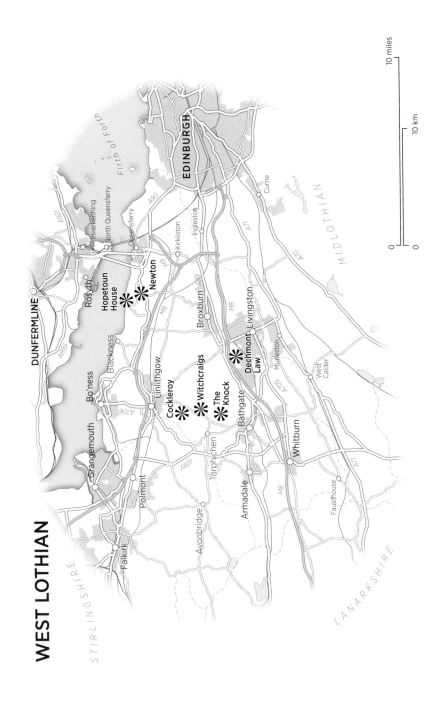

# West Lothian

## Hopetoun House

NT 088 790

Two framed paper charts set on a rooftop viewing platform. Erected by Hopetoun House Preservation Trust c.1978 and renewed in 2010. Access is by means of a staircase inside the house, which currently opens daily from Easter weekend to the last weekend of September. There is a charge for admission. The peaks identified as the Cleish Hills are the Saline Hills; the peak identified as Cullalo Hill is The Binn 191m.

> Countryside Commission for Scotland, *Eleventh Report*, 1978, p.35
>
> Personal communication, Piers de Salis, General Manager, Hopetoun House, 9 December 2010

## Newton

NT 094 779

Framed paper chart mounted on metal legs. Erected by West Lothian Council in 1998.

## Cockleroy

NS 989 743

Metal disc on a plinth of local stone. Erected by the Automobile Association and unveiled on Wednesday, 22 October 1980. Dochrie Hill 366m, Black Law 698m and Earl's Seat 578m are not visible.

> 'AA's latest viewpoint – on a clear day you can see forever', *Linlithgow Gazette*, 31 October 1980
>
> AA archive lodged with Hampshire County Council, 73M94/G1/1/848

## Witchcraigs

NS 990 727

Two laminated paper charts on a metal frame. Designed by Alasdair Hamilton of Ordie Interpretive Design, erected by the landowners Andy and Elspeth Gibbs and unveiled on Thursday, 11 September 2003. Ben Ledi and Stuc a'Chroin are misidentified; the peaks identified as the Moorfoot Hills are in the Lammermuirs.

'Excellent Outlook: New viewpoint officially opened to sightseers', *Linlithgow Journal and Gazette*, 23 September 2003

## The Knock

NS 990 711

Bronze disc on a stone cylinder. Designed by John Mathieson and erected in 1936 by Lt. Col and Mrs D.M. Sutherland J.P. The Sutherlands gave 4½ acres of land, including the Knock, to Bathgate Town Council in that year. Blackhope Scar, Dun Rig and Ben Cruachan are misidentified. None of these are visible.

'Gift to Bathgate: Highest Hill in West Lothian', *The Scotsman*, 14 March 1936

## Dechmont Law

NT 033 697

Square metal plate on a stone cairn. The plate has no information as to installer or date, and West Lothian Council was unable to provide definite answers on either point. The device is most likely to have been installed by Livingston Development Corporation c.1991 in connection with the opening of Dechmont Law Park. The peak identified as Ben Lawers is something else, probably Meall nan Tarmachan. Ben Lawers is not visible. The peak identified as North Berwick Law is Traprain Law.

Countryside Commission for Scotland, *Twenty-first Annual Report*, 1988, p.55

'Dechmont Law Park project formally opened', *West Lothian Courier*, 11 October 1991

*Retired couple examine the indicator at the Knock, near Bathgate. Photo taken 22/05/2009.*

# LANARKSHIRE

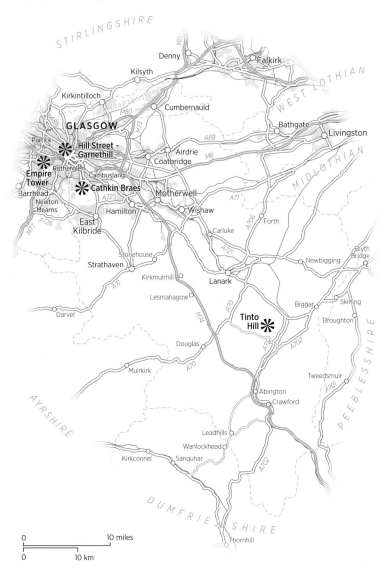

STIRLINGSHIRE

Denny
Falkirk
Kilsyth

Kirkintilloch
DUMBARTONSHIRE
Cumbernauld
WEST LOTHIAN

GLASGOW
Bathgate
Livingston

Partick
Hill Street -
Garnethill
Airdrie
Coatbridge

Empire
Tower
Rutherglen
Cambuslang
Cathkin Braes
Motherwell

Barrhead
Newton
Mearns
Hamilton
Wishaw

East
Kilbride
Carluke
Forth

MIDLOTHIAN

Stonehouse
Newbigging
Blyth
Bridge

Strathaven
Kirkmuirhill
Lanark

Darvel
Lesmahagow
Biggar
Skirling

Tinto
Hill
Broughton

Douglas
Abington
Tweedsmuir

Muirkirk
Crawford

PEEBLESSHIRE

AYRSHIRE

Leadhills
Wanlockhead
Kirkconnel
Sanquhar

DUMFRIESSHIRE

Thornhill

0 ————— 10 miles
0 ————— 10 km

# Lanarkshire

## Hill Street, Garnethill ▧

NS 581 661

Metal plate, 35½ inches by 12, mounted on the railings of a viewing platform at the west end of Hill Street. Erected by Glasgow City Council c.1997. When I visited on 23 April 2010, the plate was still in place, but the viewing platform had been closed to allow redevelopment of the site.

> Personal communication, Stewart Leighton, Glasgow City Council, 2 March 2011

## Empire Tower

NS 549 637

There was a photographic view indicator on a balcony of the 300 foot tower built on Bellahouston Hill as the centre piece of the Glasgow Empire Exhibition. When the tower opened in May 1938, Humble reported that the indicator was 'in six sections of 6 feet by 18 inches and extends round the parapet of the upper balcony'. After four months it had become 'Bellahouston's derelict indicator… all but two sections have been removed, and on these two the details of the photographs are unrecognisable because of damp'. The indicator vanished with the tower, which was demolished in 1939.

> B.H. Humble, 'View from the Tower of Empire', *Evening Times*, 4 May 1938
>
> B.H. Humble, 'Will the Tower of Empire be Retained?', *Evening Times*, 24 September 1938

## Cathkin Braes ▧

NS 618 585

Ian Fraser tells me that the indicator which originally stood here took the form of a panel on a single stone cairn. He believes it was installed in the early 1980s. The 1984 edition of the Ordnance Survey map *Western & Central Scotland* has a viewpoint symbol here.

Glasgow City Council replaced the original cairn with a much larger structure in 2005/06. This consisted of five panels, each about 25 inches by 15 inches, set on a curved stone wall. When I visited on 3 March 2010, the panels were missing; the wall remained.

In the 1930s, there was a flagstaff at this site, which Humble recommended as a location for a view indicator in several articles.

Personal communication, Ian Fraser, Glasgow City Council, 6 May 2009

## Tinto Hill

NS 953 343

Doulton stoneware disc on a cylinder of local stone with a cap of Aberdeen granite. Designed by James A. Parker at the request of the Tinto Indicator Committee and erected on Friday, 13 September 1935. As well as several residents of the nearby town of Biggar, the committee included Harry MacRobert, the president of the Scottish Mountaineering Club. Funds for the

*Tinto Hill indicator. The masons just finished on 13 September 1935. Source: London & North Eastern Railway Magazine, April 1946*

indicator were raised by an appeal in several Scottish newspapers. The stoneware slab was smashed by vandals in the early part of 1940. Visitors to the summit in 1945 and 1956 found the plinth empty. A metal disc, carrying a replica of Parker's design, was subsequently placed on the plinth but disappeared c.2004. Around 4 September 2012, the stone cylinder was rebuilt and a new metal disc installed, a joint effort by local Rotary Clubs.

'Proposed viewpoint indicator for Tinto', *The Glasgow Herald*, 18 June 1934

'Tinto Top: Erection of an Indicator', *The Scotsman*, 28 September 1935

J. A. Parker, 'The Tinto Indicator', *Cairngorm Club Journal*, Volume 14, number 77, June 1936, pp.110–114

J.A. Parker, 'The Tinto Indicator', *Scottish Mountaineering Club Journal*, volume 21, issue 123, April 1937, plate at p.222 (image of the upper surface of the disc)

'Tinto', *The Glasgow Naturalist*, Volume 14–15, 1945, p.74

J.A. Parker, 'View Indicators on Mountains', *London & North Eastern Railway Magazine*, Volume 36, Number 4, April 1946, p.80–81

Elizabeth Orr Boyd, 'On Tintock Tap', *The Scots Magazine,* Volume 65, 1956

'On the top of Tinto', photo by Kevin 76 on Flickr, dated June 2003 (shows metal disc)

Personal communication, Peter Blood, Osprey Signs, 19 January 2010

Minutes of Joint Meeting Hosted by The Rotary Club of Biggar, 4 September 2012

# PEEBLESSHIRE

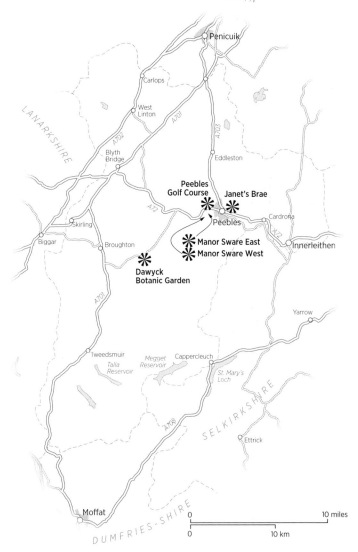

# Peeblesshire

## Peebles Golf Course NT 240 408

Marble slab on a stone cylinder. Erected by Peebles Golf Club in 1999 to mark the Millennium.

*The Millennium Cairn at Peebles Golf Course. Photo taken 17/12/2010.*

## Janet's Brae NT 268 404

Laminated panel on a stone cube. Erected by Scottish Borders Council in 2000. (The panel has no fewer than seven logos but the project was led by the council.)

Scottish Natural Heritage, *Facts and Figures*, 2000/01, p.161

Personal communication, Dr John Dent, Scottish Borders Council, 5 January 2010

Personal communication, Alistair Milligan, Ross Associates, 7 January 2010

# Manor Sware West   NT 233 397

Metal plate set on a curved stone wall. Erected by Peebles County Council c.1991/92. The plate looks towards Tweeddale. The Manor Sware indicators cannot currently be reached by car from the west, because the Old Manor Bridge has been closed to vehicles; it is still open to pedestrians. The peak identified as Broughton Heights 573m is Trahenna Hill 549m.

> Countryside Commission for Scotland, *Twenty-fourth Annual Report*, 1991/92, p.41

*One of the two metal plates mounted at Manor Sware. This plate looks towards Tweeddale. Photo taken 30/11/2009.*

# Manor Sware East  NT 237 397

Metal plate set on a curved stone wall. One of a pair with Manor Sware West. Erected by Peebles County Council c.1991/92. The plate looks towards Peebles.

# Dawyck Botanic Garden  NT 168 346

Metal plate on a wooden frame. Drawn by the architect David Mason ARIAS, and installed by the Royal Botanic Garden in the early 1990s. The garden is open daily, 1 February to 30 November; an admission charge applies.

Personal communication, Jane McCrorie, Royal Botanic Garden, 21 October 2013

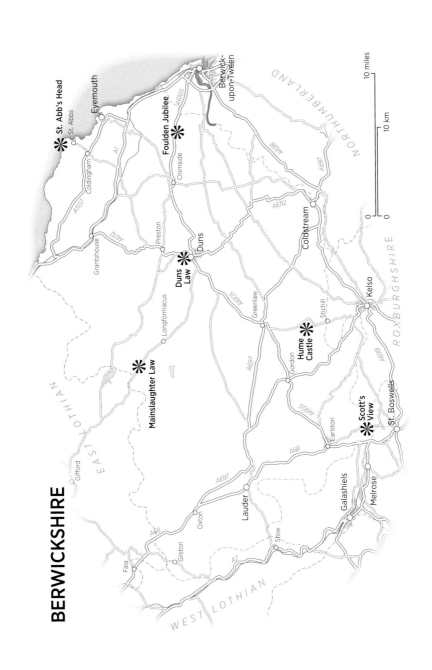

# Berwickshire

## St. Abb's Head

NT 912 691

Laminated disc set on a dressed stone cube. Erected by the National Trust for Scotland in 1986. The orientation of the disc is not ideal: the line labelled 'Bass Rock' points to a spot in the sea about half way between Bass Rock and Berwick Law.

> Countryside Commission for Scotland, *Eighteenth Report*, 1985, p.55
>
> Personal communication, Kevin Rideout, NTS, 5 May 2009

## Mainslaughter Law

NT 663 602

Metal disc on a stone cylinder. Erected by Cranshaws, Ellemford and Longformacus Community Council c.2000. Dun Law (1691 feet) is not visible.

> Personal communication, Mark Rowley, 21 February 2013

## Foulden Jubilee

NT 927 557

Framed paper chart on a dressed stone plinth. Designed by local artist Arthur Wood and erected by Foulden, Mordington and Lamberton Community Council. It was unveiled in September 2002 to mark the Queen's Golden Jubilee. The peak identified as White Law is The Curr 564m. White Law is visible in front of The Curr and below the skyline.

*The Mainslaughter Law indicator on a misty December day. Photo taken 16/12/2012.*

> 'Foulden viewpoint marks Jubilee', *Berwickshire News*, 25 September 2002 (photo of unveiling)

173

*The Foulden Jubilee viewpoint looks towards England. Photo taken 02/12/2009.*

## Duns Law                                                    NT 784 545

Metal plate on a stone plinth. Erected by Scottish Borders Council in 1999 to mark the Millennium.

> Personal communication, Dr John Dent, Scottish Borders Council, 5 January 2010

## Hume Castle                                                 NT 704 413

Bronze disc on a granite column. Designed by James Hewat Craw, erected by the Berwickshire Naturalists' Club and unveiled on Thursday, 27 August 1931. The indicator is set on the ramparts of a twelfth century castle, and is reached by a stone staircase. The castle is open from April to September during daytime.

> 'Indicator Unveiled at Hume Castle', *The Scotsman*, 28 August 1931.
> *History of the Berwickshire Naturalists' Club*, volume 27, p.306–311

## Scott's View                                                NT 593 342

Bronze plate on a stone plinth. Erected by the Automobile Association and unveiled on Tuesday, 15 May 1956. A new disc was installed on the plinth in August 1993 by Borders Regional Council and Scottish Borders Enterprise.

'Bronze Plaque unveiled on Bemersyde Hill', *The Southern Reporter*, 17 May 1956

# ROXBURGHSHIRE

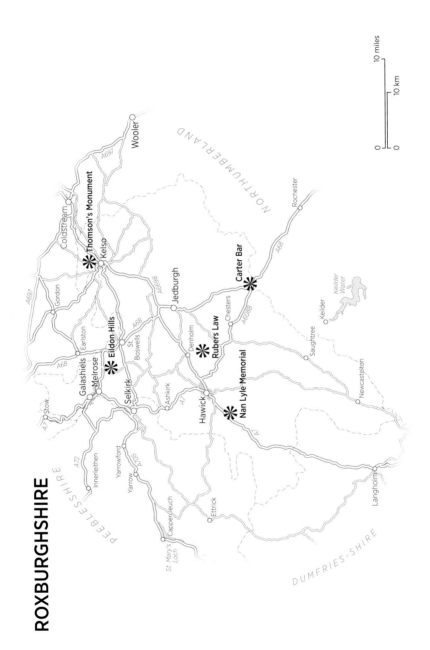

# Roxburghshire

## Thomson's Monument                                    NT 734 362

Laminated panel on wooden legs. Erected by Ednam, Stichill & Berrymoss Community Council in 2008. The panel is a few yards from a nineteenth century obelisk.

Personal communication, Alistair Milligan, Ross Associates, 7 January 2010

## Eildon Hills                                          NT 548 322

Bronze disc on a granite column. The Eildon Hills indicator was designed by John Mathieson at the request of a committee chaired by the president of the Edinburgh Sir Walter Scott Club, and was unveiled on Thursday, 2 June 1927. The idea for the scheme was that of John Clarke, a past president of the Cairngorm Club. Funding was obtained by public subscription. In October 1927, a correspondent in *The Scotsman* pointed out a couple of errors on the disc, and it was subsequently re-engraved. The disc now agrees well with digital models of the view.

John Clarke, 'The Eildon Mountain Indicator', *History of the Berwickshire Naturalists' Club*, volume 27, p.68–69 (includes diagram of face of disc)

'Eildon Mountain Indicator', *Scottish Geographical Magazine*, Volume 43, Issue 4, pp. 237–238, 1927

'Eildon Hills Indicator', *The Scotsman*, 10 May 1927

'A Mountain Indicator', *The Glasgow Herald*, 4 June 1927

'The Indicator on the Eildons', *The Scotsman*, 18 October 1927

'Eildon Indicator', *The Scotsman*, 20 October 1927

## Rubers Law                                            NT 580 155

Metal disc mounted on top of an Ordnance Survey triangulation pillar. Designed by the graphic artist Graham Anderson and erected by Borders Exploration

Group. About thirty people were present on Sunday, 4 August 2013 when Sir Michael Steel Strang unveiled the disc.

'Rubers Law' and 'The toposcope on Rubers Law' photos taken by Walter Baxter in August 2013 on Geograph

'Exploration group reaches new heights to mark 20th anniversary', *The Southern Reporter*, 30 August 2013

## Nan Lyle Cairn                                          NT 466 109

Polished granite disc on a stone cylinder. Designed by Judith Murray and Lindsey Knox, and erected by the friends and family of Nan Lyle (1929–2010). Lyle, who lived at Hawick, was an active member of many clubs including the Scouts and Borders Exploration Group. More than 140 people attended the unveiling ceremony of Sunday, 26 June 2011.

'Friends gather to celebrate unveiling of fitting tribute to Nan Lyle', *The Southern Reporter*, 17 July 2011

'Nan Lyle Cairn Unveiling', YouTube video, uploaded on 27 June 2011

## Carter Bar                                          NT 697 068

A view indicator was installed at Carter Bar by Borders Regional Council c.1982. Quentin McClaren remembers this as a steel plate mounted on a boulder on the east side of the road. This was replaced by a framed paper chart c.1995. When I visited on 1 December 2009, there were two copies of this chart at the border: one on a boulder on the east side of the road, and the other about 50 yards away on the west side. The hill identified as Hownam Law is Goshen Hill 405m. Hownam Law is the peak visible on the skyline behind Goshen Hill.

Countryside Commission for Scotland, *Fifteenth Report*, 1982, p.38

Personal communication, Dr John Dent, Scottish Borders Council, 5 January 2010

Personal communication, Quentin McClaren, Scottish Borders Council (retired)

'Southbound Layby', photo on Flickr by Alexander Cunningham dated Easter 1990

*The Nan Lyle Cairn. Photo taken 16/12/2012.*

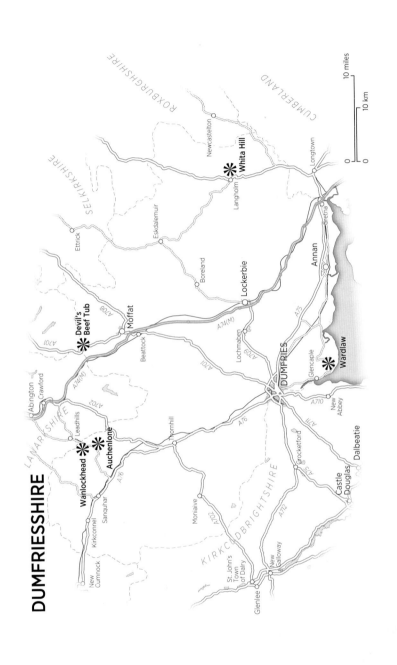

# Dumfriesshire

## Wanlockhead

NS 872 129

Framed paper chart on metal legs. Erected by Kirkconnel Parish Heritage Society in December 2006 as part of a geology trail called 'Set in Stone'.

Kirkconnel Parish Heritage Society website, kirkconnel.org

## Devil's Beef Tub

NT 060 125

Laminated disc on a stone cylinder. Erected by Moffat and District Community Council in 1984. By the time I visited on 12 May 2009, some of the wording on the disc had become difficult to read.

Countryside Commission for Scotland, *Sixteenth Report*, 1983, p.50

Personal communication, Jean Purves, Moffat and District Community Council, 15 January 2010

*Devil's Beef Tub. Photo taken 12/05/2009.*

# Auchenlone

NS 878 099

Bronze disc on what appears to be a water pipe filled with concrete. The Auchenlone indicator was erected as part of a Youth Rally attended by more than 200 young people to mark Empire Youth Weekend. The chairman of Dumfriesshire Youth Council explained to those who attended that 'such a rally could be likened to the German Strength-Through-Joy movement'. The indicator was the work of Wanlockhead Youth Club under the guidance of Mr. T.E.M. Landsborough. At the unveiling ceremony of Sunday, 21 May 1944, praise was led by Wanlockhead Youth Club Silver Band. The hill on which the indicator stands is called Auchenlone on the disc and in contemporary reports; it is East Mount Lowther on Ordnance Survey maps.

> 'Youth Rally: An Experiment At Wanlockhead', *Dumfries & Galloway Standard*, 27 May 1944
>
> 'Youth Rally at Wanlockhead and Leadhills', *The Scottish Educational Journal*, 2 June 1944

# Whita Hill

NY 379 847

Framed photograph, about 4½ feet long by 11 inches wide, mounted on wooden legs. Designed by Emma-Jane Ahart and her father Doug Malpus, and erected by the Moorland Project in 2006. The indicator is about fifty yards from a nineteenth century obelisk. Four peaks are misidentified.

> 'Launch of Langholm Moor Project is nothing to grouse about', *The Southern Reporter*, 18 September 2007
>
> Personal communication, Emma-Jane Ahart, formerly of the Moorland Project

*Labelled photograph on Whita Hill. Photo taken 05/12/2009.*

# Wardlaw

NY 024 666

Plastic covered paper chart mounted on a wooden frame. Erected by Caerlaverock Estate in 2006. It will be found next to a tree near a wooden picnic table.

Personal communication, Anna Johnson, Dumfries & Galloway Council, 21 March 2011

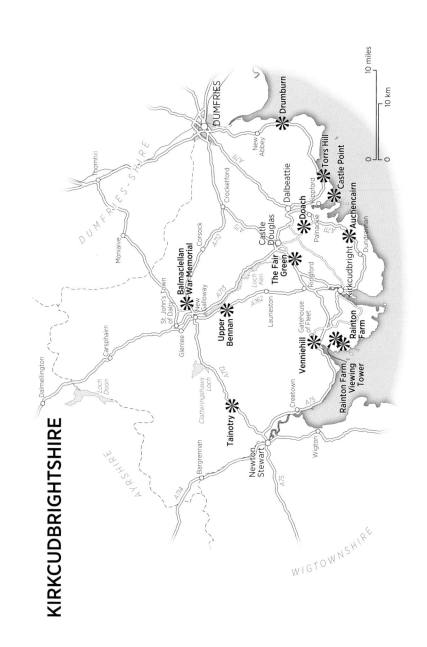

KIRKCUDBRIGHTSHIRE

# Kircudbrightshire

## Balmaclellan War Memorial 📷

NX 654 791

Framed paper chart on a stone plinth. Erected by Balmaclellan Community Council to mark the Millennium and unveiled on Friday, 3 August 2001. The photograph on the chart is by local photographer Allan Wright. Be warned that on some Ordnance Survey maps (e.g. *Landranger* sheet 84, 2007 edition) the viewpoint symbol has been placed at the top of a medieval motte whose original defences have been supplemented by barbed wire. Trying to reach this 'viewpoint' is not recommended. The chart is easily accessible.

'There'll be no trouble finding Balmaclellan', *The Galloway News*, 9 August 2001

Personal communication, Godfrey Smith of Balmaclellan

## Upper Bennan 📷

NX 650 722

Laminated panel on a stone plinth. Erected by Dumfries and Galloway Regional Council and the Forestry Commission c.1990. Some of the features shown on the panel are obscured by vegetation in summer.

Personal communication, Keith Kirk, Dumfries and Galloway Council, 1 June 2009

## Talnotry

NX 481 712

Panel on a stone plinth. Ronald Turnbull mentions a viewpoint indicator here in a 1999 guidebook. It seems most likely to have been installed by the Forestry Commission c.1972 in connection with the establishment of the Talnotry Trail. On some old Ordnance Survey maps, the site is marked by a viewpoint symbol. When I visited on 17 November 2013, the panel was missing, but the 3½ foot high plinth remained. A labelled drawing of the view appears in the Forestry Commission leaflet below.

Forestry Commission, *Talnotry Forest Trail*, 16 pages, The Galloway Gazette Press: Newton Stewart, 1972

Ronald Turnbull, *Walking the Lowther Hills*, 1999, p.141

## Drumburn 🦋 NX 980 618

Laminated panel on a stone plinth. The coloured drawing of the view to the Lake District is signed by Robin Ade. Erected by Dumfries and Galloway Council in 2004.

## The Fair Green NX 740 596

Laminated board mounted on wooden legs. Erected by the Rhonehouse Village Hall Committee in summer 2008. The board has a labelled photograph.

> Personal communication, Anna Johnson, Dumfries & Galloway Council, 21 March 2011

## Doach 🦋 NX 798 578

Framed chart set on wooden legs. Designed by Brian Stewart and erected by the Forestry Commission in 2004. The chart carries a computer generated image of the view towards the Solway Firth. The Commission told me that the 2004 chart replaced an earlier one of unknown date.

> Personal communications, Robin Fuller, 8 March 2010 and Brian Stewart, Forestry Commission

## Venniehill 🦋 NX 593 559

An indicator was erected at this site by the National Trust for Scotland c.1984 and was renewed c.2003 and again in 2013. The current device is a framed paper chart mounted on wooden legs. It is set within a circular stone enclosure a few yards in diameter. The peaks identified as Dalmalin Hill and Whinny Hill are both other objects.

> Countryside Commission for Scotland, *Seventeenth Report*, 1984, p.53
>
> Personal communication, Rhoda Davidson, SNH, 28 June 2011
>
> Personal communication, Elaine Clark, NTS, 21 October 2013 (I am grateful to Elaine Clark for supplying me with an image of the 2013 chart)

## Topps Hill 🦋 NX 887 544

Paper chart, covered with plastic, on a stone cube. Designed by Nicky Walton and installed in 1982. One of a pair with Castle Point.

# Castle Point

NX 854 524

Paper chart, covered with plastic, on a stone cube. Designed by Nicky Walton and installed in 1982. The original chart was renewed with a laminated board in 2004. All the landscape features on the chart are visible but its orientation is not ideal. The site is called Castle Point on the chart; it is Castlehill Point on Ordnance Survey maps.

# Rainton Farm Viewing Tower

NX 599 516

Four photographic panels mounted on a wooden viewing tower. Erected by Cream O'Galloway farm c.2003. The tower will be found near the farm house. Access to the top of the tower is by means of a staircase. There is an admission charge.

Personal communication, Rhoda Davidson, SNH, 24 March 2011

# Rainton Farm

NX 590 511

Plastic covered paper chart, in three sections, attached to a wooden fence. Erected by Cream O'Galloway farm c.1994. The peak identified as Culreoch is some other object.

Personal communication, Helen Fenby, Cream O'Galloway, 25 March 2011

# Auchencairn

NX 780 498

Metal disc on a stone plinth. Designed by Dumfries and Galloway Regional Council, erected by Auchencairn Community Council and unveiled on Thursday, 11 February 1993. Four natural landscape features on the disc are not visible: Lowther Hill, Merrick, St. Bees Head and the Mull of Galloway.

'Viewpoint unveiled', *The Galloway News*, 18 February 1993

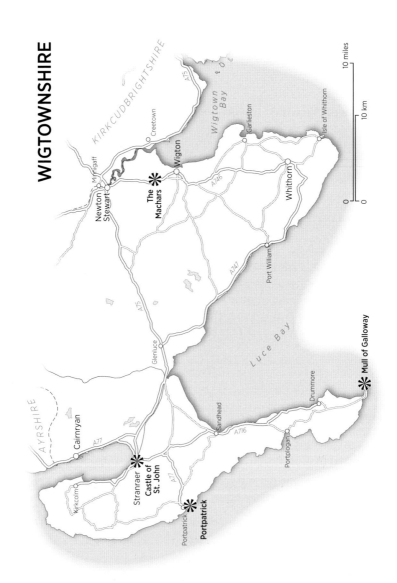

# Wigtownshire

## Castle of St. John

NX 060 608

Two panels on the tower of a sixteenth century castle. Designed by local artist Jane Fraser and erected by Dumfries and Galloway Council in 2010. Access is by means of a spiral staircase. The castle currently opens between the end of May and the end of September.

Personal communication, John Pickin, Dumfries and Galloway Council

## The Machars

NX 423 581

Laminated panel on a stone plinth. Erected by Dumfries and Galloway Council around 1995/96. The peak identified as Barholm Hill is something else, probably Kirkdale Hill.

Personal communication, Anna Johnson, Dumfries and Galloway Council

## Portpatrick

NX 000 536

Bronze disc on a concrete cylinder. The installer and date are unknown.

## Mull of Galloway

NX 156 304

Polished granite disc on a stone cylinder. Designed by James Hutchison (a geography teacher in Drummore) and erected by Kirkmaiden Community Council in 2000 to mark the Millennium. The designer told me that 'the "cairn" was built (!) when I was away on holiday and the indicator placed on top at the bottom of a hollow from which there was precious little view. To add insult to injury the disc was set with my true north being determined with a compass and so the whole thing is about 3 degrees out. To say I was disappointed is an understatement.'

At least eight of the features on the disc are not visible.

Personal communication, Steve Hardy, South Rhinns Community Development Trust, 7 February 2010

Personal communication, James Hutchinson, 5 April 2010

# SHETLAND

*UNST*

Haroldswick

Baltasound

Belmont

Gutcher

*YELL*

*FETLAR*

Mid Yell

North
Roe

Ulsta

*SHETLAND
ISLANDS*

Hillswick

Booth of Toft

A970

✳ Sullom Voe Terminal

*St. Magnus Bay*

Brae

✳ Dales Voe

*MUCKLE ROE*

Voe

*WHALSAY*

*PAPA STOUR*

Norby

Scord of
Weisdale ✳

A971

Bixter

✳ Whiteness

Walls

*FOULA*

✳ Foula

Lerwick

Scalloway ✳

Niggards

Scalloway

Hamnavoe

Brindister

*BRESSAY*

A970

Sandwick

*MOUSA*

Boddam

Sumburgh

0            10 miles

0            10 km

# Shetland

## Sullom Voe Terminal

HU 398 728

Panel on a stone plinth. Donated by the oil industry to mark the five billionth barrel of oil being exported from the nearby oil terminal on 23 December 1993.

*This panel overlooking Sullom Voe Terminal is Scotland's most northerly view indicator. Photo taken 21/06/2010.*

## Dales Voe

HU 406 682

Panel on wooden legs. Erected by Shetland Amenity Trust c.2006, the panel carries a labelled photograph of the view to the east. This is one of a series of about 50 panels with a distinctive aircraft-fin shape; four of these carry labelled landscape photographs and have been included here.

## Scord of Weisdale  HU 381 505

Panel on wooden legs. Erected by the Shetland Amenity Trust c.2006, the panel carries a labelled photograph by Panphotos, a company which is based a few miles away in Aith.

Personal communication, John Pedley, Panphotos, 1 July 2010

## Whiteness HU 402 462

Panel on wooden legs, one of the Shetland Amenity Trust series, erected c.2006. The panel carries a labelled photograph by Panphotos.

*Whiteness – one of the distinctively shaped Shetland Amenity Trust panels.*

## Foula HT 961 407

Copper disc on a Y-shaped stone shelter. A memorial to Betty Holbourn and Alasdair Holbourn. John Holbourn told me that the memorial was installed by Isobel Holbourn and her first husband Kenneth Gear in the 1980s. The copper for the disc was salvaged from the SS *Oceanic*, which was wrecked on Foula in 1914.

John Holbourn, Bradford on Avon, personal communication

# Scalloway

HU 411 396

Panel on stone cairn, one of the Shetland Amenity Trust series, erected c.2006. The panel carries a labelled photograph.

# ORKNEY

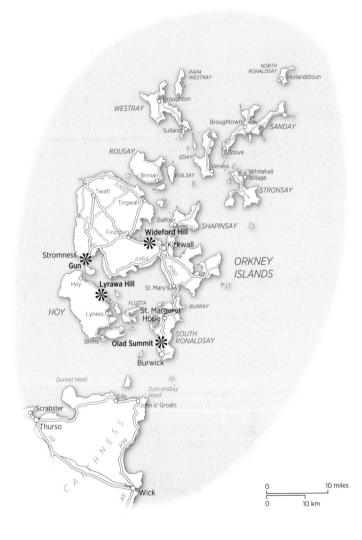

ORKNEY ISLANDS

PAPA WESTRAY

NORTH RONALDSAY
Hollandstoun

WESTRAY
Broughton

Sulland

Broughtowns

SANDAY

ROUSAY

EDAY
Stove

Brinian

EGILSAY

Veness

Whitehall Village

STRONSAY

Twatt

A966

Tingwall

Balfour

SHAPINSAY

Finstown

**Wideford Hill** ✳

**Kirkwall**

Stromness
**Gun** ✳

A964

Hoy

**Lyrawa Hill** ✳

St. Mary's

A961

**HOY**

Lyness

FLOTTA

**St. Margaret Hope**

BURRAY

Brims

**Olad Summit** ✳

Burwick

SOUTH RONALDSAY

Dunnet Head

Duncansbay Head

Gills

John o' Groats

Scrabster

Thurso

A9

C A I T H N E S S

A99

A9

Wick

0          10 miles
0          10 km

# Orkney

## Wideford Hill

HY 411 116

Metal disc mounted on a metal post. Erected by the Rotary Club of Kirkwall. The disc is dated 1968; the unveiling ceremony took place on Wednesday, 30 April 1969. Since then, a cluster of telecommunication masts, huts and fences has grown up on the summit of Wideford Hill. These largely block the view. Five of the natural landscape features on the disc are not visible even in a digital world without these obstructions.

'Where do we go from here?', *The Orcadian*, 8 May 1969

## Gun

HY 250 082

Framed paper chart on a stone plinth. Erected by Orkney Islands Council and Stromness Community Council in the early 1990s and renewed in 2007.

Personal communication, Christine Skene, Orkney Islands Council, 8 April 2010

*Gun viewpoint. Photo taken 23/03/2010.*

## Lyrawa Hill   ND 284 996

Panel on a stone plinth. Erected by Orkney Islands Council c.1991. Christine Skene tells me that the panel showed the islands that can be seen. By the time I visited on 26 March 2010 it had been stolen; the plinth remained.

Personal communication, Christine Skene, Orkney Islands Council, 8 April 2010

## Olad summit  ND 445 878

Bronze disc on a dressed stone cube. Erected by South Ronaldsay and Burray District Council in 1973. Fair Isle and Copinsay are not visible.

*Olad summit. According to an inscription, the disc was 'made by Orcadian Craftsman'. Photo taken 24/03/2010.*